1968: The Election
That Changed America

1968:
THE ELECTION
THAT CHANGED
AMERICA

Lewis L. Gould

The American Ways Series

IVAN R. DEE   *Chicago*

1968: THE ELECTION THAT CHANGED AMERICA.
Copyright © 1993 by Lewis L. Gould. All rights reserved,
including the right to reproduce this book or portions thereof in
any form. For information, address: Ivan R. Dee, Inc., 1332
North Halsted Street, Chicago 60622. Manufactured in the United
States of America and printed on acid-free paper.

Library of Congress Cataloging-in-Publication Data:
Gould, Lewis L.
    1968 : the election that changed America / Lewis L. Gould.
      p.   cm. — (The American ways series)
    Includes bibliographical references and index.
    ISBN 1-56663-009-6 (cloth : alk. paper). — ISBN 1-56663-010-X
(pbk. : alk. paper)
    1. Presidents—United States—Election—1968. 2. Elections—
United States—History—20th century. 3. United States—Politics
and government—1963–1969. I. Title. II. Title: Nineteen sixty
eight. III. Series.
JK1968   1968
324.973'0923—dc20   92-35614

Contents

The Johnson peace initiative. Nixon and South Vietnam. The Humphrey surge and Nixon's response. The election results and their meaning.

Preface

By the 1990s public disenchantment and anger with politics in the United States had reached intense levels. Huge budget deficits, a persistent economic slowdown, and unmet social problems focused popular unhappiness on the political system and its flaws. A generation of divided government, in which Republicans dominated the presidency while Democrats controlled Congress, produced an apparent gridlock in Washington which stalled constructive responses to the nation's needs. Angry voters flirted with third parties or grew apathetic toward politics altogether.

The origins of these problems extended back into the mid-1960s when the Democratic party waged an unpopular war in Vietnam, pursued a Great Society in domestic affairs, and dealt with long-deferred issues of civil rights for black citizens. By 1968, however, the war in Vietnam had become stalemated. Liberal programs to improve the lives of the poor and minorities provoked bitter opposition among white Americans. As a result, the presidential election of 1968 became a contest in which the passions and violence of the society surged into the political arena. Assassinations, urban rioting, and war added new volatility to national politics.

The outcome of the election left no one fully satisfied. The Republicans put Richard Nixon in the White House, but the Democrats retained control of both houses of Congress. Radicals were frustrated that the nation had not

embraced social revolution. Conservatives resented the residual strength of liberal ideas. The issue of race had not been
addressed nor its effects diminished. A close election had left
things much as they had been when the year began—or so it
seemed on the surface.

In fact, the 1968 election proved to be a watershed
event in American politics. Republicans used the skills they
brought to Nixon's campaign to create an ascendancy in
presidential politics. Democrats, divided and torn after 1968,
emerged as only crippled challengers for the White House
in the 1970s and 1980s. Bitterness over racial issues and
discord on the Vietnam War continued to shape national
affairs. The events of 1968 changed the way Americans felt
about politics and their leaders. An erosion of confidence in
American institutions began that has not yet reached a
conclusion.

Soon after Nixon took office, books appeared to explain
the trauma through which the country had passed. Since
those early accounts, historians and journalists have reexam-
ined 1968, most often in the context of the rebellious college
students who rallied to liberal Democrats such as Eugene
McCarthy and Robert F. Kennedy. Few authors have considered the political history of the whole election, including the
crucial events of the last month of the campaign. The
analytic narrative that follows provides an overview of the
election based on the many published works on the campaign and unpublished materials at the Lyndon B. Johnson
Library.

Like most Americans in 1968, I experienced the events of
that year through television. It was a time of recurrent
shocks, intense emotions, and passionate judgments. Twenty-
four years later I have tried to examine the election in a calm

and judicious spirit. During a troubled time, fallible men and women made decisions that changed the nation. This book considers the reasons for actions and events that occurred during the critical 1968 election and the lasting consequences for American politics and society.

Acknowledgments

I WANT TO thank John Braeman and Ivan Dee for inviting me to contribute to the series of which this volume is a part. Both of them also offered helpful and thoughtful criticisms of earlier drafts. At the Lyndon Baines Johnson Library, Linda Hanson and Claudia Anderson provided their customary efficient and timely assistance. David Humphrey of the Library directed me to information on the Vietnam negotiations of October 1968 that proved important for the final chapter.

My interest in this election grew out of an essay on Lyndon Johnson and the Democratic party that Robert A. Divine asked me to write. Herbert F. Margulies of the University of Hawaii provided informed and incisive comments on the entire manuscript. Students in seminars on Lyndon Johnson and his times helped me to work out ideas on the politics of the 1960s. Karen Gould was a constant source of encouragement through her own scholarly writings and through her good spirits and personal courage.

L. L. G.

November 1992
University of Texas at Austin

1968: The Election
That Changed America

Introduction

THE PRESIDENTIAL ELECTION of 1968 was a decisive event in recent American political history. After its victory in that contest, the Republican party dominated the White House, winning four of five presidential races by wide margins in the popular and electoral votes. For Democrats, the picture at the presidential level turned bleak after 1968. Only in 1976, with the Southerner Jimmy Carter at the head of their ticket, were they able to squeeze out a narrow victory over Gerald Ford and the Republicans; Ford was arguably the weakest GOP candidate since Barry Goldwater in 1964. During the two decades that followed the 1968 race, Republicans set the agenda for American political life. The result was an ascendancy of conservative ideas and programs in the creation of national policy.

Until the mid-1960s Democrats were the political party of change and innovation. Starting with Woodrow Wilson during the Progressive Era and continuing at an even greater rate with Franklin D. Roosevelt and the New Deal of the 1930s, Democrats expanded the role of the national government in domestic and foreign policy. Roosevelt's Democratic successors, Harry Truman, John F. Kennedy, and Lyndon B. Johnson, saw themselves as extending and elaborating the Roosevelt legacy. Democratic power rested on an electoral base of a majority of American voters who made up what was called the New Deal coalition. As one Democrat noted during the 1960s, his party was comprised of "the liberal-labor-Negro coalition that has elected every liberal president and made possible every liberal advance since the 1930s." To most members of the party, Democrats were the natural governing organization of the nation. After all, with the exception of Dwight D. Eisenhower's eight years as president, Democrats had by 1964 controlled the White House for twenty-four of the preceding thirty-two years.

Between 1964 and 1968 the Democratic party lost ground. A number of elements accounted for this political decline. The presidential leadership of Lyndon B. Johnson alienated many voters who recoiled from the Great Society's domestic programs, the Democrats' racial liberalism, and the impact of the war in Vietnam. Within four years after Johnson's smashing triumph over Barry Goldwater and the Republicans in 1964, Democrats were beleaguered and discredited. Late in 1967 Postmaster General Lawrence F. O'Brien surveyed the condition of his party and reported to President Johnson, "The Democratic party, to a greater or lesser extent, has lost contact with the voters."

While Democrats floundered during the mid-1960s, Republicans rebuilt their organization after the debacle of 1964. The GOP was not as weak as it appeared at the time of Goldwater's defeat. Its base in the Midwest and Far West gave it the electoral resources it needed to survive a reverse such as 1964 and to regroup and wait for Democratic difficulties. In addition, despite Goldwater's national defeat, Republicans had won five Southern states in 1964. With the erosion of Democratic support under Johnson, Republicans were poised by 1968 to regain the electoral dominance they had lost during the 1930s.

Complicating the Republican task in 1968 was the presence of a viable third-party candidate in the South in the person of the former governor of Alabama, George C. Wallace. A talented demagogue, Wallace had a knack for articulating the resentments and fears of white Americans, North and South, in rhetoric that assailed both major parties with equal venom. Both Republicans and Democrats were forced to conduct two-front political campaigns in 1968 to stave off the strong threat posed by Wallace to the two-party system.

Most writing on the 1968 election has focused on the exciting events of that turbulent year—Lyndon Johnson's withdrawal in March, the assassination of Martin Luther King, Jr., in early April and the killing of Senator Robert F. Kennedy in early June, and the tumultuous Democratic National Convention in August. These sensational occurrences made the election seem at the time a contest primarily for the soul of the Democratic party. The issue seemed to be how liberal the United States would be in the future. The outcome of the election showed that the Democrats had indeed lost touch with the country.

Such a possibility would have seemed improbable to Democrats during November 1964. Lyndon Johnson had led the party to a sweeping triumph over the Republicans. The president carried all but six states and swamped Goldwater in the electoral college, 486 to 52. The gap in the popular vote total between the winner and the loser was 16 million ballots. And Johnson's coattails were long and powerful: Democrats controlled the House of Representatives by 290 to 145 and the Senate by 68 to 32. The question was whether Republicans had become a permanent minority party which could no longer mount a credible challenge.

The Democratic triumph was brief. Within two years Republicans rebounded strongly and proved that their obituary had been premature. In the 1966 congressional elections the GOP gained forty-seven seats in the House and three in the Senate. They added eight governorships to those they already controlled, including the key state of California where newcomer Ronald Reagan achieved a decisive success. Richard Nixon recalled that his party had "been the recipients of a massive anti-Johnson windfall." What had happened in two years to transform Democratic triumph into a Republican comeback that presaged the party's return to the presidency in 1968? The presidential election of 1968 was determined in large measure by the decline in Democratic fortunes that occurred between 1964 and 1968.

The most significant electoral issue in 1968 was not the Vietnam War, which attracted most of the attention during the campaign. The most determining subject on the minds of voters was race. The gains of blacks during the period 1960–1968 had aroused powerful resentments among the white population. Urban riots, student protests, and the rise of the Black Power movement further alienated whites. The result was an electoral reaction against Democrats that has remained a powerful element in national politics ever since. A direct link may be noted between the character of the Nixon and Wallace campaigns in 1968 and the subsequent Republican campaigns of Ronald Reagan and George Bush. It makes the 1968 election a decisive episode in modern American political history.

1

On the Eve of 1968

THE PRESIDENTIAL ELECTION year of 1968 began in a poisoned atmosphere of social tension and political bitterness. "I think that 1968 is going to be the worst year that any of us has seen here," said a British journalist based in New York as the New Year opened. American columnists and reporters echoed his gloomy prediction. "There is a sharp sense of crisis in the American air, spreading and souring," wrote Emmet John Hughes in *Newsweek*. Hughes found "a tension in society and a stress among men—not known since the 1930s."

The most immediate source of the pervasive unhappiness in the nation was the war in Vietnam. Since Lyndon Johnson had intensified the American commitment in Southeast Asia in 1965 with the bombing campaign against North Vietnam and the introduction into South Vietnam of large numbers of combat troops, the conflict had raged on with greater loss of life on both sides and with no tangible military gains. Almost half a million American soldiers were in Vietnam by the end of 1967. Casualties among Americans in the fighting had reached 150,000, with 20,000 deaths since 1961. The number of dead and wounded among the Vietnamese population stood in the millions. More and more Americans—over 40 percent in one poll—regarded the war

as a mistake. Antiwar protests were growing in size and
intensity during the autumn of 1967. Demonstrators became
more and more pointed in their denunciation of the man
they saw as responsible for the endless carnage:

Hey, hey, LBJ
How many kids
Did you kill today?

As the cruel rhyme indicated, Lyndon Baines Johnson
aroused passions almost as heated as those surrounding the
war. As 1968 opened Johnson was entering the fifth year of
his presidency. He had come to the White House upon the
assassination of John F. Kennedy on November 22, 1963.
During his first eighteen months in office the president had
been a legislative dynamo, pushing through legislation and
advocating the creation of a "Great Society" which would
conquer poverty and injustice. He had beaten Barry Goldwater decisively in the 1964 presidential election and seemed
to stand atop American politics as his full term began in
1965.

Despite his huge electoral triumph, Johnson was still a
mystery to many Americans. He had been a congressman
from Texas for eleven years and then won a disputed—some
said "stolen"—election to the Senate in 1948 by an eighty-
seven-vote majority. "Landslide Lyndon" rose rapidly in the
Senate and became Majority Leader in 1955. Legislative
successes, including the Civil Rights Act of 1957, gave him a
prominence among national Democrats. He made an abortive race for the Democratic nomination in 1960 and then
was named John F. Kennedy's running mate. His years as
vice president were unhappy ones, and rumors were heard
that he might not be on the ticket in 1964. Then came
Dallas and he was president.

Johnson seemed larger than life in the early days of his presidency. He was everywhere—on the phone to lawmakers, cajoling reporters, exhorting the nation to do great things. In the sad aftermath of John Kennedy's death, he seemed a figure of calm authority who adeptly managed the transition of power. His political appeal was one of "moderate and prudent" leadership, in the words of one newspaper correspondent. With his election to the presidency at stake, he sought "to preempt the high ground, the moderate thoroughfare, the middle of the road from his Republican opponents." The Lyndon Johnson whom Americans saw in 1964 was as dignified and restrained a man as it was possible for him to be.

Another, less attractive Lyndon Johnson emerged during the three years that followed. He treated staff members with a mixture of sadistic cruelty and benevolent paternalism that became legendary in Washington. To the press he was alternately solicitous and carping. He loved to deceive reporters in ways large and small. In an era before it was seemly to say that the president lied, Johnson became known for his "credibility gap." As a reporter for *Time* put it, "He cannot stand affronts and regards his occasional critics as treasonous."

Johnson yearned to win the affection and trust of the American people, but the task proved beyond his powers. He had an essential insecurity at the center of his personality that prevented him from trusting the American people to sustain his policies on their merits. A close adviser, Joseph Califano, observed correctly that Johnson "learned too late that the manipulative and devious behavior commonplace in the back alleys of legislative politics appalled the American people when exposed in their President." Johnson once asked a friend why people didn't like him. The answer was, "Mr. President, you are not a very likeable man."

These qualities hampered Johnson even more as a war-time president. American involvement in Southeast Asia was already substantial when John F. Kennedy was killed. Presidents Truman, Eisenhower, and Kennedy had committed the United States to oppose Vietnamese communism and after 1954 to support the new country of South Vietnam that had been created when France withdrew as a colonial power. During the Kennedy administration the number of American military "advisers" in South Vietnam rose from six hundred to sixteen thousand men at the time of the president's murder. Johnson had a valid if typically overstated point when he said in 1965 that "since 1954 every American president has offered support to the people of South Vietnam."

But Lyndon Johnson's presidential decisions had propelled the United States into the major combat phase of the war in Vietnam, and it became his major political problem. If he took credit for the legislative accomplishments of his administration in domestic affairs, he could not evade responsibility for the Vietnam War that had become a foreign policy failure by late 1967.

Johnson had asked Congress for authority to make bombing strikes after North Vietnamese naval vessels allegedly attacked American ships in the Gulf of Tonkin in 1964. He had decided to bomb North Vietnam on a sustained basis in early 1965, and later that year had sent large contingents of combat troops to South Vietnam. To most of the American public, the war, whatever its origins, had become "Lyndon Johnson's War."

The president had been unable to offer a convincing rationale for U.S. involvement in this Asian conflict. He had also failed to provide a clear statement of how Americans would know when victory had been achieved. These political troubles grew out of the confused purposes within the Johnson administration itself. There the war in Vietnam was seen as part of a larger confrontation between an expansionist communist campaign, masterminded by the Soviet Union and Communist China and working through the North Vietnamese, and the forces of Western democracy seeking to preserve the independence of South Vietnam. At the same time Washington recognized that South Vietnam lacked the internal cohesion and national will to defeat its enemy. The United States aimed to overcome this political weakness through the use of its military power until South Vietnam could stand on its own. Many observers believed that the American presence undermined a faint South Vietnamese nationalism and defeated the very goal it sought to achieve. The United States was thus trying to defend a country that seemed to lack the resolve to defend itself.

The Johnson administration also underestimated the will and determination of North Vietnam. Bombing raids were designed to inflict sufficient pain on Hanoi so that they would either abandon efforts to subvert South Vietnam or agree to a negotiated political settlement. North Vietnam believed, however, that the United States lacked the will for a prolonged war. "Americans do not like long, inconclusive wars," said one North Vietnamese leader, "thus we are sure to win in the end." On their side, the North Vietnamese had Russian and Chinese logistical support, an agricultural country that bombing could injure but not destroy, and each year a hundred thousand young men who turned eighteen. Lyndon Johnson was fighting an enemy with the means and the will to conduct a long war. The administration could not supply a credible prediction of success.

All the Johnson White House could offer to the people of the United States by 1967 was continued bombing of targets in North and South Vietnam, a steady increase in American dead and wounded on the battlefield, and an elusive promise that just a little more sacrifice and effort would show positive results. By the autumn of 1967 the patience of the American people with Johnson's policy was running out. On both sides of the war issue sentiment increased for an end to the fighting. Advocates of peace, often called "doves," clamored for a negotiated settlement. Supporters of the war, labeled "hawks," asked why the war could not be won since the United States was expending so much blood and treasure.

The focus of the discontent over Vietnam was Johnson himself. Even Democrats now accused him "of the most monstrous character failings imaginable" in the conduct of the war. "He's got this Texan policy of shoot first and ask questions afterward," said one liberal critic. Republican Governor Ronald Reagan of California charged Johnson with wasting American lives in the war: "He must take responsibility for the policy of war and what the results of that policy are." Reagan's answer was more vigorous prosecution of the fighting. By October 1967 the president's public approval rating as a war leader had fallen to a record low 31 percent. Johnson told a reporter a few months earlier: "Our biggest problem is not with Ho [Chi Minh, the North Vietnamese leader] and with the fighting out there. It's with our situation here. It's leading the enemy to believe that we might quit."

Damaging as the Vietnam War was for Lyndon Johnson and the Democrats, it did not approach the impact on the American voter of an even more volatile domestic problem—the race issue. By August 1967 the White House was receiving public opinion polls indicating that "racial problems" were "the number one concern of 8 out of 10" of those surveyed. Taken during a period of urban rioting that marked the summer of 1967, this poll tracked other evidence of the same public mood. During 1966 surveys had said that three-quarters of the white electorate thought that blacks were moving ahead too fast. White voters contended that blacks demanded too much at the expense of whites. Organized labor discovered after Democratic losses in the 1966 congressional elections that many union members "deserted liberal candidates for one reason only: in protest against their advocacy of civil rights."

The civil rights record of Johnson's presidency was impressive. It included the Civil Rights Act of 1964, which gave all citizens equal access to public facilities irrespective of their race and outlawed racial discrimination in education and in the workplace. Next came the Voting Rights Act of 1965, which removed barriers to voting in the South. In the minds of Southern whites, the Johnson administration also implemented these policies vigorously. More than any other president before him, Johnson had identified his administration with the aspirations of blacks. In September 1966 he said that "20 million of our Negro fellow citizens have the power of the United States government behind their right to vote for the first time in the history of this land."

By 1967, however, the Democratic record on civil rights had become a political liability. To militant blacks who advocated a stronger attack on racism, Johnson was at most an untrustworthy friend. At the other end of the political spectrum, many white voters saw the Johnson administration as sacrificing their interests on behalf of blacks who responded to federal programs and money with violence and rioting. Two British politicians visiting the United States during the election of 1966 informed an aide of Hubert Humphrey's that "in district after district, and city after city, they found an undercurrent of resentment concerning civil order and gains made by the Negro population."

A number of forces had produced this unhappy condition for the Democrats. Inside the civil rights movement, the nonviolent tactics of Dr. Martin Luther King, Jr., had proved less effective in dealing with racial conditions in Northern cities such as Chicago. Champions of a more assertive style of protest had gained national attention with calls for "Black Power" and a degree of separatism from white society. Beginning with riots in the Watts district of Los Angeles in 1965 and continuing in the "long, hot summers" of 1966 and 1967, urban violence had become part of the unfolding story of black protest against their disadvantaged place in American society. The result was a high degree of apprehension among whites about the direction of the civil rights movement and a mounting resentment at what they perceived as ingratitude among blacks for the sacrifices whites had made on their behalf.

In the popular mind, the state of race relations became linked to protests against the war in Vietnam. The resulting social trauma was seen as evidence that the Johnson administration was insensitive to issues of "law and order" and unwilling to take a tough stand against domestic dissent. The president was responsible for both prompting the protests and then for allowing them to continue. "Disturbances and demonstrations are lumped together," said a White House memorandum, "and the blame for these civil disorders is placed on the Administration."

The issue of crime and citizen safety also worked against the party in power. During the 1960s the incidence of violent crimes, murder, rape, assaults, and robberies had increased at an alarming rate. Over the first six years of the decade, the number of reported crimes went up by more than 60 percent while population grew only 10 percent. The rate at which blacks were arrested for homicide rose by more than 130 percent between 1960 and 1970. Campaigning for president, Richard Nixon charged that during the Johnson administration "crime and violence have increased ten times faster than the population." These alarming allegations oversimplified a more complex reality to which demographic shifts, the availability of firearms, and the tensions of urban living contributed. Nonetheless, the crime issue became a continuing burden for the Johnson White House and the Democrats.

One popular explanation for the rising crime rate was that liberal judges imposed restrictions on police officers in the conduct of their duties. The U.S. Supreme Court, led by Chief Justice Earl Warren, received primary blame or credit for this situation. The Court's decision in *Miranda v. Arizona* (1966), requiring police to inform a suspect in a criminal case of his right to remain silent during questioning, symbolized what many believed to be an undue sensitivity to the rights of criminals rather than their victims. In fact, the *Miranda* decision did not frustrate the police to the extent that its critics charged, but the perception during the 1960s was that it did. Judges whom Lyndon Johnson had nominated for the Supreme Court, particularly his old friend Abe Fortas, were the focus of conservative criticism for their rulings on criminal procedures. Fortas's role in the *Miranda* case, said Senator Sam Ervin of North Carolina, had allowed "multitudes of murderers, rapists, burglars, robbers, and thieves to go unwhipped of justice." The law-and-order issued nagged at Democrats all during the 1968 campaign.

On the surface the economy should not have been a problem for the White House as the presidential race neared. Unemployment during 1967 had been around 4 percent, and inflation was running at under 3 percent annually. The projected deficit in the federal budget for 1968 would be more than $11 billion. Although economic activity had been sluggish in 1967, the economy was still enjoying the boom of the 1960s. Defense spending on the Vietnam War was further accelerating economic growth.

In the politics of 1968, however, these optimistic figures masked a more sober reality. Although inflation was still small compared to what the 1970s and 1980s would bring, the rise in prices worried voters, and they told pollsters that it was their "most urgent problem." The projected budget deficit was quite large by the standards of the time, and Republicans charged that it reflected the distorted priorities of the Johnson administration in advancing domestic programs during wartime. There were also fears for the stability of the dollar in international markets during 1967–1968. The balance of payments was running against the United States, and gold was leaving the country. The financial impact of the war in Vietnam was disrupting the federal budget, unleashing inflation, and calling into question how President Johnson was managing the economy.

The administration also encountered substantial economic discontent among the nation's farmers. In May 1967 the White House was told by one of Hubert Humphrey's aides that the Democrats would likely lose "every non-southern state with a farm-voter population of 9% or more." The agricultural community in the Midwest complained that their expenses rose constantly while the prices they received for their crops had fallen off since 1966. They charged that during a time of prosperity "people out in the country are earning lower incomes than big-city minority slum dwellers." Farmers blamed the Johnson administration for "holding down consumer food prices at the farmer's expense." When the White House endorsed cheaper food prices and the president urged housewives not to buy expensive butter, Democrats suffered in the farm belt.

Added to these substantive issues was the Democrats' organizational disarray after four years of Johnson's political leadership. Although the president had a reputation as a masterful politician, in fact he had little interest in the affairs of the party machinery. The Democratic National Committee had withered during his presidency. Its chairman, John Bailey of Connecticut, was a figurehead; Johnson kept real power in his own hands. He shifted fund-raising to large contributors and allowed the party's base of small contributors to dry up. Almost no attention was paid to such basic matters as voter registration and mobilization. Seeking to be a nonpartisan president, Johnson made appointments in many states without regard to party affiliation, to the dismay of committed Democrats in his party. As Postmaster General Lawrence O'Brien reported to Johnson in September 1967, the result was that "many of the state organizations are flabby and wedded to techniques which are conventional and outmoded." In addition, "The Democratic National Committee is not staffed or equipped to conduct a successful presidential election."

So striking were Lyndon Johnson's political problems in late 1967 that he faced the unusual situation for an incumbent president of an important challenge to his renomination. By December 1967 Johnson had a declared opponent in the field against him and another potential rival of even greater political significance. The announced contender was Senator Eugene J. McCarthy of Minnesota, who had become a candidate on November 30. He said he would enter several primaries in order to "challenge the President's position" on

Vietnam, and he argued that his campaign did not represent "any great threat to the unity and strength of the Democratic party." The other possible rival was Senator Robert F. Kennedy of New York, brother of the late president. In the later months of 1967 Kennedy had been seriously weighing a race against the president but had decided not to make the run under the existing circumstances.

When McCarthy announced, the political consensus was that he posed no serious threat to Lyndon Johnson's renomination in 1968. How could a relatively obscure senator from the upper Midwest defeat an incumbent president for renomination? When the McCarthy campaign got off to a slow start, that conventional wisdom was reinforced. By mid-December 1967 a White House aide informed the president with amusement that "Eugene McCarthy is doing so badly that I am tempted to float a rumor that he is actually working for you to dispirit the 'peace movement.'" Reports from around the country supported a discounting of McCarthy's campaign.

In fact, the McCarthy revolt against the president represented a more important political threat than the White House realized. Throughout the early months of 1968 most political observers underestimated McCarthy's capacity as a candidate. This misjudgment grew out of his mixed record as a senator since 1958. Fifty-two years old in 1968, McCarthy had won election to the House of Representatives in 1950 and served four terms. In 1958 he ran against a popular Republican for the Senate and won a large victory in the Democratic landslide that year. He was an effective liberal legislator in his first term. His talents led Johnson to consider him closely as a vice-presidential possibility in 1964; as a liberal and a Catholic, McCarthy would have balanced the ticket well. In the end, Johnson decided that Hubert

Humphrey had even better claims on the position because of his liberal accomplishments and standing within the Democratic party. The process by which Johnson led McCarthy on and then dumped him in favor of Humphrey left some scars with the senator who was a proud, even conceited, figure. Surveying the possible Democratic candidates in 1960, for example, McCarthy had quipped, "Why don't they just nominate me? I'm twice as liberal as Humphrey, twice as Catholic as Kennedy and twice as smart as [Stuart] Symington." For a man of McCarthy's self-esteem, to be turned down in favor of his Minnesota colleague whom he regarded as inferior was a wound that smarted for years. "He really felt he was led down the primrose path," a relative later recalled.

McCarthy's willingness to challenge Johnson in 1968 did not rest simply on a personality conflict with the president. It also arose from McCarthy's reservations about the wisdom of the administration's Vietnam policy and the view of the presidency that Johnson advanced to support his actions. An initial break came during 1965 when the administration intervened in the Dominican Republic to put down an ostensible communist government in that Latin American country. By January 1966 McCarthy was also attacking the Vietnam War. So serious was the commitment of American military power, he said, that it required "a national debate, a national discussion, and a real searching of the mind and soul of America." He did not move to outright opposition to the president until 1967. On February 1 he told an audience at a peace mobilization in Washington that in the absence of positive reasons for supporting the conflict "we must be prepared to pass harsh and severe judgment on our position in this war." Four weeks later he called the war "morally unjustifiable."

Several elements led McCarthy to this position. His daughter Mary was a convinced opponent of the fighting, and she had a strong influence on her father's thinking in 1966 and 1967. The actions of the Johnson administration, and its constitutional rationale for the war, also troubled the Minnesota senator. He doubted the argument that China needed to be contained, and it bothered him when the Gulf of Tonkin resolution of 1964 was invoked to justify the president's policy. After Undersecretary of State Nicholas Katzenbach called the resolution the "functional equivalent" of a declaration of war, an angry McCarthy told a reporter, "There is no limit to what he says the president can do. There is only one thing to do—take it to the country." A suspicion of imperial presidents and their actions would be a significant theme in McCarthy's campaign in 1968.

By early 1967 McCarthy was beginning to think about mounting a challenge to Johnson, if only to provoke a debate on the wisdom of the Vietnam policy. The most formidable obstacle to such a move was Senator Robert F. Kennedy of New York, the heir apparent to his brother's political legacy. If Kennedy decided to run against Johnson, McCarthy's chances would disappear. During the autumn of 1967, however, it seemed that Kennedy was reluctant to go up against an incumbent president, and opponents of Johnson turned to other alternatives. McCarthy's possible candidacy took on new allure.

Within the left wing of the Democratic party there had been rumbles all during 1967 of challenging Lyndon Johnson's candidacy. The leading proponents of what became the "Dump Johnson" effort were two opponents of the war, Allard K. Lowenstein and Curtis Gans. Lowenstein had been active in liberal causes since his college days and had participated in the Adlai Stevenson campaigns of the 1950s.

During the 1960s he had played a role in civil rights campaigns and was an official of the Americans for Democratic Action (ADA). Gans was also a member of the ADA and had earlier been connected with the more militant Students for a Democratic Society (SDS). In July 1967 Gans made Johnson the target of an insurgent political movement which would run candidates against him in the 1968 primaries. If all went well, Gans contended, Johnson might conclude to withdraw from the race, as President Harry S Truman had done in 1952. During the remainder of the summer and into the fall, Lowenstein and Gans used a shadow organization, the Conference of Concerned Democrats, to find an alternative to the president. They found stirrings of support among liberal Democrats opposed to the war.

Their first choice was Robert Kennedy, but the New York senator declined after a series of meetings in September and October 1967. "People would say that I was splitting the party out of ambition and envy," Kennedy told them. Other possibilities, including Senator George McGovern, stood aside. In mid-October Lowenstein went to see McCarthy and found to his surprise that the senator was willing. "Somebody has to raise the flag," McCarthy remarked. Six days later, in a meeting with Lowenstein and another liberal leader, McCarthy made his decision definite. "You guys have been talking about three or four names. I think you can cut the list down to one now."

McCarthy proved to be a formidable candidate, but he did not seem so at first. His second term had not been a distinguished one in the Senate, in part because he had become bored with the routine of the place. His voting record on several issues revealed vulnerabilities that his opponents would exploit during 1968. He had supported the oil depletion allowance that favored the oil industry; his civil rights record was solid but seemed to lack the emotional sympathy that Robert Kennedy now displayed on this issue. He wanted to run for president in his own way and on his own terms. The McCarthy campaign was always disorganized and confused, and in his formal speeches the candidate rarely stirred his listeners.

On the other hand, McCarthy's understated style was highly congenial to the group within the Democratic party that remembered with affection the campaigns of Adlai Stevenson. There was about McCarthy much that appealed to the liberals in the suburbs who expected candidates to make rational arguments on serious issues. His laconic wit also evoked memories of John Kennedy's personal style. The senator drew on the support of independents and some Republicans who responded to his wry, literate speeches and his detached, ironic approach to political life. He was uncomfortable asking for the votes of Americans on the basis of ethnic affiliation or economic position. His constituency, he said, was "a constituency of conscience."

McCarthy intended to run in four primaries—Massachusetts, Wisconsin, Oregon, and California, states where his antiwar message would have the greatest electoral appeal. Supporters urged him also to run in the New Hampshire primary on March 12, 1968, but throughout December 1967 the senator weighed the wisdom of such a move. On January 3 he announced he would enter the New Hampshire contest. The chairman of the Democratic National Committee warned the White House that the McCarthy forces would pose a real threat to the president in both Massachusetts and New Hampshire.

For Lyndon Johnson and the men around him, McCarthy's opposition was less of a threat than the possible challenge from Robert Kennedy. The president and the New York senator had long detested each other. Their animosity went back at least to the 1960 campaign when Kennedy had managed his brother's presidential race in a manner that alienated Lyndon Johnson. During Johnson's time as vice president, their dislike for each other had intensified. Johnson's assumption of the presidency in 1963 had been followed by a year of uneasy collaboration in which the two men had maintained a façade of public unity. The president rebuffed efforts to have Kennedy become his running mate, but he supported his former attorney general's Senate candidacy in New York. During 1965 and 1966 Kennedy moved cautiously away from his endorsement of Johnson's policy on Vietnam. In early 1967 he came out against the bombing of North Vietnam and called for negotiations with Hanoi to seek a resolution of the conflict.

Kennedy was the logical leader of the antiwar forces within the Democratic party. Only he had the electoral appeal to mount a credible challenge to Johnson's candidacy for renomination. If he ran, he would evoke the memory of his assassinated brother. Moreover, he seemed able to draw into his campaign a wider variety of groups than any other candidate. Kennedy's standing with black Americans, the young, and the disadvantaged led many Democrats to regard him as a potential healer for the tensions roiling American society. It was an alluring vision for many in the party who dreamed that such a coalition might ensure a Democratic victory in the fall.

The New York senator was a shrewd enough politician to recognize the weaknesses of his possible candidacy. In the South he was an object of hatred among many whites, and his candidacy in Dixie would be hard to sustain. Within Democratic ranks he had a well-deserved reputation for

playing hardball politics, and a challenge to Johnson would
be seen as further confirmation of his limitless ambition. If
he went up against the president and lost, he would impair
his chances for a future race for the White House. Kennedy
had been hit hard by his brother's death, and he was
reluctant to take on the rigors of a presidential contest with
its dangers and burdens for his family. Dislike of Johnson
and the Vietnam War impelled him to run, but caution
stayed his hand. "In his gut, he wanted to go," a friend
remembered. "He felt it was the right thing to do, but his
judgment told him his chances of success were so slim, it
wasn't the right decision."

So when Lowenstein and Gans approached Kennedy in
the autumn of 1967, he turned them down. It was a
significant mistake. Kennedy had judged that Johnson
would remain politically strong and that no other Democrat
could mount a credible opposition to the president. When
McCarthy entered the race, it suggested that the Minnesota
senator had the courage to run while Kennedy, the exponent
of moral values and passion in politics, stood aside. The
contrast that young people and antiwar activists drew between the two men did not please Kennedy, but he continued
to believe as 1968 opened that he should stay out of the
presidential race.

On the eve of the presidential contest in 1968, the Democratic party stood in feeble condition. Its electoral base was
tottering, its hold on the voters was slipping, its internal
organization was chaotic. Many voters disliked Johnson. The
policies of his administration had made converts for his
partisan opposition. As a result, Johnson's candidacy in 1968,
as yet unannounced, had already drawn one potentially
credible rival in Eugene McCarthy. Meanwhile, Robert Kennedy waited just offstage.

Victory for the Democrats in 1968 rested, party members told one another, on the anticipated mistakes of the Republicans. In this comforting scenario the GOP would nominate Richard Nixon, a sure loser. Second, the presence of George C. Wallace of Alabama as a third-party candidate would "drain enough votes from the Republicans to elect Johnson." In essence, the Democrats would not have to win the 1968 election. Their opponents would lose it.

The Republican party did not intend to be so obliging. The election of 1964 had been a political debacle for the GOP. As a Republican governor put it in December 1964, "We have suffered a defeat as severe in quality and quantity as any that the Republican party has ever sustained." In addition to losing the presidency, the Republicans had dropped 38 seats in the House of Representatives to stand at 140 members, lowest since 1936. In the Senate they had lost two seats and had only 32 members, which put them where they had been in 1940. More Republican defeats in state and local contests prompted talk of eventual disappearance of the party from the American political scene.

Republican rebuilding began with the selection of a new chairman of the Republican National Committee in January 1965. Ray Bliss was a veteran party leader from Ohio where he had assembled an effective statewide organization. In 1960 Bliss's skill had enabled Richard Nixon to carry Ohio against the popularity of John F. Kennedy. Still, the task he confronted when he took over the RNC in early 1965 was staggering. The Goldwater defeat had left the party in disarray, though there was some good news on finances because of late contributions received by the party in 1964. Bliss persuaded the holdover Goldwater supporters on the committee to leave, and he turned to fund-raising on a sustained basis. Success on the financial side was immediate as party contributors, small and large, poured in enough money to make the Republicans competitive in the 1966 elections. Bliss also stressed organization rather than ideology and gradually rebuilt the party's organizational base. He allowed the Republican Coordinating Committee, composed of officeholders and party leaders, to frame alternatives to Johnson's programs. Bliss stressed the issue of inflation, and that bread-and-butter subject became a chief element in the Republican rebound.

Events also worked for the Republicans. The popular reaction against Great Society programs in 1965 and 1966 made the electorate more sympathetic to the Republican message. Most significant were the issues of race and crime. In a September 1966 poll 52 percent of Americans thought the Johnson administration was moving too fast on civil rights.

The 1966 congressional elections indicated how the Johnson administration had lost ground among voters. Republicans picked up forty-seven seats in the House of Representatives and gained three senators and eight new governors. The number of Americans identifying themselves as Republican rose from 25 to 29 percent, reversing twenty years of decline. New GOP faces appeared—Charles S. Percy won a Senate seat in Illinois when he defeated a liberal stalwart, Paul H. Douglas; Spiro Agnew became the new governor of Maryland; and in California the popular and attractive Ronald Reagan trounced the Democratic incumbent, Edmund G. "Pat" Brown. Republicans were no longer political invalids; they were credible challengers to Lyndon Johnson and the Democrats in 1968.

The next step for Republicans, however, was more difficult: they needed a nominee to run against Lyndon Johnson in the presidential race. The ostensible front-runner after 1966 was the governor of Michigan, George Romney. Elected to three terms in a key industrial state, Romney was a handsome, imposing figure on television. A former automobile executive and a devout Mormon, he seemed to have an appealing blend of business experience and executive ability. Reporters familiar with his career in Michigan wondered how well his ponderous speaking style and slow-moving mind would fare on the national scene. Another potential contender was Nelson A. Rockefeller, governor of New York. Barry Goldwater's main opponent in 1964, Rockefeller had incurred the hatred of the party's conservative wing for his attacks on their hero. Finally, a third governor was Ronald Reagan, whose victory in California had been large and impressive. A staunch supporter of Goldwater, Reagan had already shown an ability to captivate conservative audiences, and his advisers were eyeing a race for 1968.

The most formidable entry in the Republican race was a man who had been widely regarded as a political has-been only a few years earlier. Richard Milhous Nixon was fifty-three in 1966; he had been an important participant in American politics for a decade and a half. After eight years as Eisenhower's vice president he lost the 1960 presidential election to John F. Kennedy in a close and hard-fought contest. Attempting a comeback two years later by running for governor of California, he lost again to Edmund G. Brown, Sr. Some in the press wrote Nixon's political obituary. In 1964 he remained loyal to Goldwater when other Republicans such as Rockefeller bolted the party. Once Johnson's policies faltered, Nixon was ready to court the Republican faithful once again. In 1966 he campaigned eagerly for party candidates across the country, amassing the credits he would turn into delegate votes in 1968.

So successful had Nixon been on behalf of Republicans in 1966 that Lyndon Johnson attacked him personally on the eve of the congressional elections. Johnson called Nixon "a chronic campaigner" after the Republican criticized his Vietnam policy. Nixon exploited this opportunity skillfully. He styled it "one of the most savage personal assaults ever leveled by the President of the United States against one of his political opponents," adding that Johnson's comments were those of a "very, very tired" man. The exchange reminded voters of Nixon's stature among Republicans and enabled him to treat the party's election victory as something of a personal triumph as well.

During 1967 Nixon assembled a campaign operation that was efficient and well financed. While the candidate stepped back from politics for the first half of the year and made a series of foreign tours, the men around him framed a strategy for the campaign ahead. Nixon's main problem was his image as a "loser," derived from the 1960 and 1962 defeats. He decided he had to contest the Republican primaries to prove his appeal to the voters. Meanwhile, his standing in the polls against the president improved.

By late 1967, moreover, one of Nixon's potential rivals, George Romney, had mortally wounded himself politically. In a television interview after a trip to Vietnam, Romney was asked about how his position on the war had changed. He replied that "when I came back from Vietnam, I just had the greatest brainwashing that anybody can get when you go over to Vietnam, not only by the generals but also by the diplomatic corps over there." As the episode became public, it suggested that Romney's brain was not up to the job of being president. Soon his campaign began to falter for lack of support and money. Polls by the Romney campaign in December 1967 showed him trailing Nixon by more than fifty percentage points. The Romney presidential bid was over, and on February 28, 1968, he took himself out of the race.

Two potential threats remained for Nixon as 1968 opened. If Nelson Rockefeller entered the contest, his money and energy might win some Republican support. But the men around Nixon were confident that Rockefeller lacked the strength among Republican partisans to make a serious challenge. More formidable was the new Republican governor of California, Ronald Reagan. While he had pledged to voters during his gubernatorial race that he would not run for the White House, he had not said he·would refuse a draft. During 1967 a number of conservative political operatives began putting together a Reagan-for-President campaign. Already a popular speaker before Republican audiences, Reagan spent much of the year on the banquet circuit with his five-by-eight cards that carried his prepared text. His one-liners delighted his audiences: "You have to admire the Administration's crime program. They're making the money so cheap it's not worth stealing." If Reagan entered the race directly, he could give the Nixon campaign some anxious weeks.

If the 1968 election had simply matched the Republican and Democratic candidates, it would not have produced the complexity and passion that prevailed throughout that tumultuous year. What helped to set this presidential race apart was the presence of a serious third-party candidate, the former governor of Alabama, George Corley Wallace. Wallace's talent for exploiting the racial tensions within the electorate and articulating the grievances of middle-class and lower-middle-class white voters made him a force which confounded the plans and projects of Republicans and Democrats alike. Wallace did not inject the race issue into the 1968 contest, but he used it with explosive effectiveness.

George Wallace had served as governor of Alabama from 1963 through 1967. In his inaugural address he had proclaimed, "Segregation now! Segregation tomorrow! Segregation forever!" and he had tried to block the efforts of the federal government to integrate his state's colleges and universities. In one celebrated and well-publicized episode, he stood in the door of a building at the University of Alabama to bar black students from entering. Federal marshals made sure the students were admitted, but Wallace received nationwide notoriety for his tactic. By 1964 he had decided to run in some Democratic primaries to test his strength as a national candidate. To the surprise of many observers, he achieved respectable totals—34 percent of the vote in Wisconsin against President Johnson, 38 percent in the Indiana primary, and 43 percent in Maryland. In the wake of Johnson's landslide, worries about the "white backlash" that Wallace represented receded for a time, but the governor of Alabama was simply biding his moment until the 1968 race.

First he had to overcome a problem in his home state. Alabama law barred the governor from seeking a second term. Efforts to persuade the Alabama legislature to change the state constitution failed. Wallace got around the constitutional obstacle by having his wife, Lurleen, run to succeed him. After her election in November 1966, Wallace and the men around him turned to the formidable task of mounting a serious third-party challenge. He raised about a million dollars of campaign funds during the first half of 1967, then sent his operatives to California to begin the difficult process of persuading voters in as many states as possible to put his name on the ballot. These efforts cost Wallace about half a million dollars, but by early 1968 he had succeeded. Across the South there was popular enthusiasm for the Wallace cause, and in all states in the North there was enough support to ensure that he would appear on the ballot.

What was Wallace's message in 1968? Race, he told reporters, was not the issue that drove his campaign. "There isn't any backlash among the mass of people against anybody because of color. There's a backlash against big government in this country," he said in 1967. To cheering audiences he would proclaim, "Our lives are being taken over by bureaucrats, and most of them have beards!" Wallace was careful not to make an overtly racist appeal, but the language he used conveyed an unmistakable message to white audiences. On the volatile issue of school busing, he assured the people, "When I become President there won't be one thin dime available from Federal funds to pay for all this school busin'—you can rely on that." For the members of the lower middle class in the North, "the average man in the street, the man in the textile mill, this man in the steel mill, this barber, the beautician, the policeman on the beat," Wallace was a candidate who spoke to their anxieties and fears. As a New York construction worker put it, there should be "one law for the Negro *and* the working man *and* the rich liberals. I think Wallace will do that."

The United States approached the presidential election year of 1968 in a condition of unusual political turbulence and uncertainty. Racial turmoil, economic unease, and the war in Vietnam had raised such tensions within the country during 1966 and 1967 that the presidential contest became an outlet for venting the accumulated frustrations of the decade. The American political system was about to endure a year that would test the strength and durability of its institutions. In the process, the nature of national politics would undergo long-lasting changes.

2

The President Withdraws

On March 31, 1968, Lyndon Johnson concluded a television address to the nation with the stunning announcement that he would not accept his party's nomination for president. Since that event several theories have emerged to explain why the most political president of his time suddenly abandoned national politics during an election year. The interlocking natures of Johnson's health, the war in Vietnam, and the political challenges he faced within his own party all played their part in the president's decision to step aside.

The question of his health during a second full term had long been on Lyndon Johnson's mind. He believed that male members of his family rarely lived past sixty-five—which he would be in August 1973. The heart attack he had suffered in 1955 demanded that he live prudently, but there was always the possibility of another attack. Johnson's health was also uncertain in other respects. He suffered from gall bladder problems in 1965 and had an operation for skin cancer later in his presidency. His wife, Lady Bird, doubted whether he could survive another term. When Johnson had talked about not running in 1964, just before the Democratic National Convention, she had urged him to continue in the race. By 1967, however, she was becoming convinced that another term would subject him to dangerous health risks. She feared he might be stricken in office as Woodrow Wilson had been in 1919.

Discussions between husband and wife about a withdrawal from politics became intense during the autumn of 1967. As 1968 began they returned to the issue during a visit with Texas Governor John Connally and his wife at the president's ranch in Texas. For a time Johnson planned an announcement at the close of his State of the Union address on January 17, 1968. Either by accident or design, the president failed to bring the statement with him, and the moment passed.

Johnson later said he probably would not have read the withdrawal statement anyway—it would have been a discordant note amidst his call for sacrifices in Vietnam and in domestic policy. The political situation also may have struck Johnson as more favorable to his administration and reelection than had been the case for several months. His poll ratings had improved since November. The campaign of Senator Eugene McCarthy had started very slowly. A poll commissioned by the White House showed the president with a seventy-percentage-point lead over McCarthy in one late December survey. Another poll gave McCarthy only 12 percent support in January. Antiwar Democrats complained that the McCarthy "campaign is a disaster"; the candidate's speeches were "dull, vague, and without either balls or poetry."

Johnson also had some reason for confidence in the outcome of the November election. He learned on the afternoon of the State of the Union speech that the next Gallup poll would show him "with a big lead over Reagan, Romney and Nixon and a six-point lead over Rockefeller." Even though John Connally urged him to make the withdrawal announcement because "the longer you wait the more difficult it becomes," Johnson decided to wait a little longer.

The president had miscalculated; events soon turned against him. Four days after the speech the battle of Khe Sanh broke out near the Demilitarized Zone (DMZ) in South Vietnam. Johnson followed the fighting closely, believing the engagement might be a climactic battle of the war. Then, on January 23, 1968, the North Koreans captured the USS Pueblo, an intelligence vessel, on the high seas with its crew of eighty-three men. Bogged down in Vietnam, it seemed that the United States might be facing still another military confrontation. In Congress there was pressure to retaliate.

The most devastating military development of 1968 for Lyndon Johnson came on January 31. Across South Vietnam the North Vietnamese and their guerrilla supporters in the South launched what has become known as the Tet offensive. Americans saw vivid television footage of the United States embassy under assault in Saigon, American dead lying in the streets of their ally, and house-to-house fighting near American bases. For Americans these were troubling images after constant reassurances from the Johnson administration about the prospects of victory.

The North Vietnamese offensive was defeated with heavy losses to the enemy—casualties in the tens of thousands—and their hopes for a popular uprising in the South went unrealized. In domestic political terms in the United States, the military outcome of the Tet offensive was less significant than the shock it inflicted on American public opinion. Media coverage suggested that the nation had suffered a worse military defeat than was in fact the case.

The White House failed to depict the fighting as a

setback for the enemy. As Senator George Aiken, a Vermont Republican, said of the administration's efforts to lessen the impact of the battle, "If this is a failure, I hope the Viet Cong never have a major success." More ominous for the president was the campaign remark of Senator McCarthy: "Only a few months ago we were told that 65 percent of the population was secure. Now we know that even the American embassy is not secure." A week later Senator Robert Kennedy offered an even more somber assessment. The enemy in Vietnam had "finally shattered the mask of official illusion with which we have concealed our true circumstances from ourselves."

The Tet offensive shifted the ground of American politics. In New Hampshire the McCarthy campaign gathered momentum as both defenders and opponents of the war turned against the president's policies for their own reasons. As it turned out, New Hampshire proved to be receptive to McCarthy's appeal once Johnson seemed vulnerable. It was a small state with relatively few Democrats, and these could be reached by the kind of intensive, personal campaign that McCarthy was mounting. By early February the candidate had at his disposal an army of student workers who had poured into the state to defeat Lyndon Johnson. Shaving their beards to be "Clean for Gene," young men spread out for door-to-door canvassing that played to the love of personal contact among the New Hampshire voters. The theme of their canvass was not explicitly antiwar. Instead the McCarthy campaign said, "New Hampshire can bring America back to its senses."

The Johnson campaign in New Hampshire played into the hands of the McCarthy forces. Relying on the Democratic party organization in the state, the Johnson people enlisted the support of Governor John King and Senator

Thomas McIntyre. A prominent businessman directed the Johnson campaign. To preserve the fiction that the president was not yet an official candidate, the Johnson forces worked to obtain write-in votes for him. As a means of tracking the allegiance of Johnson voters, his campaign managers came up with the idea of a "pledge card" that registered voters could fill in. Each card was numbered; one section went to the White House and another to the Johnson headquarters. The McCarthy campaign immediately charged that the pledge cards interfered with a secret ballot. The Johnson forces further overreached themselves when their campaign ads claimed that a vote for McCarthy was a vote for the North Vietnamese leader Ho Chi Minh. The reporter Charles Bartlett warned the president that McCarthy could get "a sympathy vote" if "these irritations accumulate."

A reminder of the nation's domestic difficulties appeared at the end of February. In response to urban riots in the summer of 1967, Johnson had named a national commission, led by Mayor John Lindsay of New York and Governor Otto Kerner of Illinois, to probe the causes of unrest. The Kerner Commission issued its report on February 29 and spoke of a nation "moving toward two societies, one black, one white— separate and unequal." The president's reaction to the report was restrained; he indicated he "did not agree with all of the recommendations" of the panel. Johnson's response led Robert Kennedy to conclude "that he's not going to do anything about the war and he's not going to do anything about the cities either."

Two days before the New Hampshire voting, the *New York Times* reported that General William Westmoreland, commander of United States forces in South Vietnam, was asking for 206,000 more troops. According to the *Times*, the request had set off "a divisive internal debate" within

the administration over whether or not to meet the request. The story was accurate, and the argument within
the White House would prove important in Johnson's subsequent withdrawal from the campaign. Coming when it
did, however, the *Times* story suggested that the administration was as likely to escalate the American commitment
as to reduce it.

The result in New Hampshire surprised Washington.
Although Johnson emerged the winner with 27,243 votes to
23,280 votes for McCarthy in the Democratic primary, the
closeness of the race was unexpected. McCarthy also received
some 4,700 votes in the Republican primary while Johnson got 1,778 Republican votes. Among the Democrats,
Johnson's percentage of the vote was 49.4 percent while
McCarthy received 42.2 percent. For an incumbent president
seeking reelection, a narrow victory over a relatively unknown challenger was a surprise. McCarthy won twenty of
the twenty-four delegates at stake in the primary because the
Johnson campaign, confident of victory, had put up more
delegate candidates than places available. The more focused
McCarthy campaign took the bulk of the national convention delegates. McCarthy had exceeded the expectations that
the press had established for his campaign; Johnson had
failed to live up to his reputation as a skillful politician. The
New Hampshire results punctured the illusion that Lyndon
Johnson was an unbeatable choice for the Democratic nomination.

The Republican primary outcome was more decisive.
Richard Nixon achieved an overwhelming victory with
84,005 votes to Nelson Rockefeller's 11,691. After George
Romney's withdrawal from the race on February 28, 1968,
the Nixon camp had feared that the significance of their
candidate's showing might be ignored. Instead, the triumph

helped to dispel the "loser" image that had dogged Nixon since 1962. It showed that he was a broad popular choice among Republicans who wanted to win in 1968. Earlier the press had viewed Rockefeller as Nixon's main competition because of the New York governor's good showing against Johnson in the polls. In fact, few conservative Republicans outside the Northeast had any stomach for Rockefeller. Nixon's most serious rival was the still unannounced Ronald Reagan.

During the New Hampshire primary Nixon began to evolve his own position on the Vietnam War. During a speech on March 5 he said he would offer "new leadership" to "end the war and win the peace in the Pacific." The press concluded that Nixon had a "secret plan" to end the war in Vietnam. Nixon had avoided being that explicit, but he did suggest that "the war can be ended if we mobilize our economic and political and diplomatic leadership." What he had in mind were diplomatic overtures by the United States to the Soviet Union and China to achieve a negotiated solution. Meanwhile, American troops would be gradually withdrawn and more fighting left to the South Vietnamese. Beyond that Nixon refused to go, he said, because he did not wish to interfere with Johnson's foreign policy or tie his own hands if and when he became president. The position had enough ambiguity in it to satisfy critics of Johnson on both the left and the right, which was what Nixon intended.

The furor over Nixon's Vietnam program somewhat obscured the campaign themes he was developing in New Hampshire. He criticized those who led urban riots and urged action to forestall "planners of violence." As his rationale for providing new leadership, he cited "rampant lawlessness" and "racial strife" as well as economic decline and the war in Southeast Asia. Americans had "learned the hard way that a society that is lenient and permissive for criminals is a society that is neither safe nor secure for innocent men and women."

During the New Hampshire race Nixon also put in place the campaign style he would continue through the fall election. Still bitter at his treatment by the press during his 1960 race against John F. Kennedy, and determined to prevent the media from influencing his themes, he and his aides gave few press conferences and relied on staged events aimed at the television cameras. Nixon made particularly adept use of question-and-answer sessions with ordinary citizens. In the process he convinced some journalists that a "New Nixon" had emerged, a cooler and less impulsive man than the candidate of the 1950s and early 1960s. As one of his aides said, "It's not the man we have to change, but rather the *received impression.*" Nixon's success in this transformation would be an important element in his victory in 1968.

In the aftermath of New Hampshire many attributed McCarthy's strong showing to displeasure with the Johnson administration's Vietnam policy. There was some truth in this conclusion, but the anti-Johnson sentiment did not reflect support for the dovish position on Vietnam. One preelection poll indicated that "40 percent of those declaring for McCarthy also favored escalation" of the war. Many Democratic voters were registering a protest against the president for not *winning* the war in Vietnam; they were not against the conflict itself. Unhappiness with Johnson as a national leader and the "social issues" of race and crime were other elements in the vote against him.

The New Hampshire primary made Eugene McCarthy a credible national figure among Democrats. His campaign seemed likely to acquire that elusive quality of momentum that can be so important in a presidential race. He had already shown strength in other states where liberal Democrats were strong. In Massachusetts there was no one on the primary ballot other than McCarthy; Johnson had decided not to contest the state. As a result, McCarthy picked up the state's entire delegation of seventy-two votes. Similarly, his forces ran well in caucuses in Minnesota and were poised to play a prominent role in that delegation. A large turnout of petition signers put McCarthy's name on the primary ballot in California on March 14. The morning after the New Hampshire primary Senator McCarthy told the press, "I expect to win in Wisconsin.... I think I can get the nomination. I'm ahead now."

McCarthy had no time to savor his good showing in New Hampshire. In exceeding press expectations he changed the nature of the 1968 race among the Democrats. In particular, Senator Robert F. Kennedy now faced a painful choice. During the fall and winter of 1967 he had declined offers to do what McCarthy had done. He had allowed the Minnesota senator to make what seemed to be a feckless race in New Hampshire, and now McCarthy was poised to become the choice among Democratic liberals. While Johnson might still be renominated, at the very least McCarthy was likely to emerge from 1968 as the leader of the party's left wing. Even before New Hampshire the New York senator had been reassessing his refusal to get into the race. As McCarthy's chances improved in New Hampshire, Johnson's electoral vulnerability became more evident. Kennedy began to gather information about entering other primaries and to consider what a presidential race would involve. He had to act by March 18 if he wished to enter the delegate-rich California primary.

The week of the New Hampshire primary saw a flurry of negotiations and maneuvers among leading Democrats. On Wednesday, March 13, the day after the vote, Kennedy told reporters he was "actively reconsidering the possibilities that are available to me." That afternoon, in an awkward meeting with McCarthy at the Senate, the two men, who did not like each other, agreed to carry on separate campaigns.

At the same time some Democrats, working on Kennedy's behalf, began looking for a face-saving way for him to make his point without getting into the presidential contest. Mayor Richard Daley of Chicago and Kennedy aide Theodore Sorensen proposed the idea of a commission of prominent Americans not connected with the administration's Vietnam policy who would review the war situation and make recommendations for future action. Sorensen raised the issue with Johnson on March 11, and after the New Hampshire primary the president asked for a list of those who might serve. Kennedy and Sorensen then met with Clark Clifford, the secretary of defense, on Thursday, March 14, to examine the proposal. The senator said that if the president named individuals who reflected "a clear-cut willingness to seek a wider path to peace in Vietnam," he would not run for president against Johnson. But part of the price for such a declaration would be a statement from the president that his policy in Vietnam "had proved to be in error."

Clifford told the two men that Johnson could not agree to such a statement, and he reminded his visitors that Johnson would probably be nominated, that Johnson could control the foreign policy situation by stopping the bombing or opening negotiations with Hanoi, and that a decision to run on Kennedy's part would guarantee a Republican victory.

After Kennedy and Sorensen had left, Clifford laid the idea before Johnson. There was no chance it would be accepted. It would have required Johnson to admit that Robert Kennedy was right and he was wrong, that his Vietnam policy had collapsed, and that he could no longer function fully as president. The commission idea was rejected.

The Kennedy camp also tried to work out an accommodation with McCarthy before the announcement of the New York senator's candidacy. Senator Edward Kennedy flew to Wisconsin to meet with McCarthy to propose a joint anti-Johnson effort. McCarthy showed no interest in such an endeavor which would inevitably have found him carrying the bags of the more charismatic Kennedy. His old animosities against the Kennedys welled up. "That's the way they are," he told his wife Abigail. "When it comes down to it, they never offer anything real."

On Saturday, March 16, Robert Kennedy announced his candidacy for the Democratic presidential nomination in a setting designed to evoke memories of his dead brother's 1960 campaign. The place was the caucus room in the Old Senate Office Building where John Kennedy had announced. The language of the declaration had some of the same intensity: "I do not run for the Presidency merely to oppose any man but to propose new policies." Although he was now running against the expansive foreign policy that his brother had endorsed in 1960, there was some of the same elevated rhetoric. "At stake is not simply the leadership of our party or even our country," Robert Kennedy said, "it is our right to moral leadership on this planet."

Kennedy's death by an assassin's bullet in June 1968 has cast a retrospective glow over his last campaign. Viewed in a calmer way, it is hard to see how he could either have gained the Democratic nomination or won a general election as his party's choice. In the spring of 1968 there were parts of the country, such as Texas, where he was literally a hated man. He could not enter a sufficient number of primaries to win a majority of delegates at the national convention. And in the states where he was a likely loser in November, Democratic leaders would not have turned to him against Hubert Humphrey. As was true of other Democrats who ran for the White House in 1968, Robert Kennedy's personality played as much of a role as political calculation in his decision to seek the presidency. His feud with Lyndon Johnson had to come to a showdown.

The reaction of the McCarthy camp to Kennedy's announced candidacy was predictable outrage at having their man usurped by someone who had been too cautious to run just a few months earlier. One columnist suggested that Kennedy had "come down from the hills to shoot the wounded." The near victory in New Hampshire had changed the McCarthy campaign from a protest candidacy to one that believed in the outside possibility of actually winning the nomination and the presidency. Like Kennedy, Eugene McCarthy had not rationally calculated his chances of accomplishing such a feat. The ability to carry Minnesota in Senate races, to win a Democratic primary in New Hampshire or Wisconsin, did not necessarily translate into a viable national candidacy. In negotiations with him before Kennedy announced, McCarthy had said that he was interested in only one term in office as part of "my effort to depersonalize the office" of the president. All Democrats in 1968 seemed to have a sense that whoever won the nomination would have no difficulty at all defeating Richard Nixon or any other Republican in the autumn. The problem of winning a majority of the electoral vote played little part in the political calculations of leading Democrats during the first six months of 1968.

Johnson reacted to Kennedy's announcement with strident language. Addressing the National Farmers Union on March 18 in Minneapolis, he said of North Vietnam: "We ought not let them win something in Washington that they can't win in Hue, in the I Corps, or in Khe Sanh. And we are not going to." The next day, speaking to a foreign policy conference in Washington, he added, "There is no cheap or no easy way to find the road to freedom and the road to order. But danger and sacrifice built this land and today we are the number one nation. And we are going to stay the number one nation."

The president's bellicose rhetoric struck a discordant note. His old friend James Rowe told him, "Everyone has turned into a dove." Within the Democratic party sentiment spread toward changing the nation's policy on the war. Moving ahead to increase the military commitment in Vietnam was an unpleasant alternative for many Democrats. "The prospects of a large-scale escalation are threatening to bring down the house," warned a California leader. In Wisconsin, whose primary would be held April 2, the tide was running strongly against the White House. Voters there had concluded, reported the state Democratic chairman, that "within the present context, the war in Vietnam cannot be won, the government of South Vietnam does not enjoy any substantial support from the people and South Vietnam does not represent a viable political entity worth defending." Without immediate deescalation, the president was told, "this Administration cannot survive politically."

If the perception spread in mid-March 1968 that Lyndon Johnson and his administration sought to pursue their Vietnam policy and to intensify the American commitment, the reality at the White House was quite different. In the aftermath of the Tet offensive, conflicting pressures within the Democratic party and the administration had begun to work a change in the president's policy. The key figure in the process was the new secretary of defense, Clark Clifford. Later in 1967 Johnson had become disillusioned with Robert S. McNamara, who had been secretary of defense since 1961. After McNamara sent Johnson a November 1 memorandum that outlined his growing doubts about the conduct of the war, the president nominated him to be president of the World Bank. Johnson offered Clifford the position of secretary of defense two months later on January 18, 1968. He made no mention to Clifford of any plans to step down as a presidential candidate. The sixty-one-year-old Clifford came to the cabinet with a reputation as a shrewd political operator gained from service in the Truman administration, to John F. Kennedy, and as a high-priced Washington lawyer. His political instincts were well developed, and he was a clever bureaucratic infighter. He had expressed reservations about the initial escalation of the war in 1965 but from that time forward had supported Johnson's policy. The Senate confirmed Clifford as secretary of defense on January 30, the day the Tet offensive began. The event had a decisive impact on the new cabinet officer. He wrote later, "My faith in our ability to achieve our objectives within an acceptable period of time was shaken and began to erode."

For Clifford and others who had become dubious about continuing the existing policy in Vietnam, a campaign now ensued to move President Johnson away from further escalation and toward negotiation and a limit to the American commitment in Southeast Asia. During February 1968 the

administration discussed available options. From these deliberations came Westmoreland's request for 206,000 additional
troops during 1968. There were military problems with such
an increase, but the economic and political implications of
the proposal were equally serious. To fund such a further
buildup would require a budget increase of up to $12.5
billion during 1968 and 1969. That amount would have
devastating effects on inflation and would require new taxes
in an election year or the equally unpopular option of wage
and price controls. Johnson also feared that funding for his
Great Society programs would be endangered if military
spending rose. What's more, reaching the strength that
Westmoreland wanted would mean calling up the reserves
and increasing draft calls. Such moves would undoubtedly
be politically explosive and could lead to further protests
across the nation. Americans would be asked to make new
sacrifices for a policy that still could not supply a clear sense
of when victory might be reached. One Midwestern politician warned that a call-up of the reserves, for example,
would be "political suicide at this time."

The final stages of Johnson's decisions on Vietnam and
his own political future took shape during the two weeks
after Robert Kennedy entered the presidential race on March
16. The White House had begun to prepare a speech that
Johnson would make on Sunday, March 31, about his Vietnam policy and future actions in the war. On March 18
Johnson made his hawkish speech in Minnesota. A worried
Clifford proposed that the president reconvene a group of
senior advisers from outside the government, known as the
"Wise Men," to review the situation in Vietnam. They
would meet on March 25, six days before the president's
speech.

Although Secretary of State Dean Rusk and Clifford were

now arguing for a halt to the bombing of most of North
Vietnam, Johnson still seemed convinced of the need to
continue fighting. He wanted peace language out of the
speech. "Let's just make it troops and war," he said to his
speech writers. There the matter rested for the next five
days. On March 22 Johnson announced that Westmoreland
would leave his command in Vietnam to become army chief
of staff on July 2. Three days later the Wise Men came to the
White House.

These fourteen senior statesmen, including former Secretary of State Dean Acheson, Supreme Court Justice Abe
Fortas, General Maxwell Taylor, and Arthur Goldberg, ambassador to the United Nations, read documents and heard
briefings during their stay. When they met with the president on March 26, McGeorge Bundy, a former assistant to
both John F. Kennedy and Johnson, reported the majority's
feeling "that we can no longer do the job we set out to do in
the time we have left, and we must begin to take steps to
disengage." Others disagreed, including Justice Fortas, but
the weight of opinion was on the side of limiting the
American commitment and pursuing policies to extricate the
nation from Vietnam. As Johnson said in his memoirs, if the
Wise Men "had been so deeply influenced by the reports of
the Tet Offensive, what must the average citizen of the
country be thinking?"

By late March 1968 Lyndon Johnson faced a decisive
moment in his political career. His position within the
Democratic party had further deteriorated since Robert
Kennedy had entered the race. Reports from Wisconsin
forecast a sizable victory for McCarthy in the April 2
primary. One operative reported, "It's just brutal." When the
McCarthy campaign opened a storefront headquarters, "volunteers just pour in. We open one and we're lucky to get

two people." On March 28 James Rowe sent Johnson a memorandum titled, "Is the President Running?" Politicians and reporters were deluging him with questions about Johnson's intentions. "This kind of talk has extremely bad effects on the troops in the field," Rowe concluded. The Kennedy forces were saying that the president would not run and that the best course for Democrats was to "Stay loose and stay uncommitted."

The next day the balance shifted. Clifford had suggested that Johnson's speech writer, Harry McPherson, prepare a draft that took a softer line on Vietnam. The draft went to the president late on March 28, and when he went over the speech on Friday, March 29, he used the language from McPherson's "peace" speech. Later that day, as advisers polished the draft, the question arose over a proper ending to the speech. When McPherson proposed to prepare a new conclusion, Johnson told him, "I may have a little ending of my own."

On Saturday, March 30, Johnson called his former speech writer, Horace Busby, who three months earlier had advised the president not to run. Johnson asked him, "What do you think we ought to do?" Busby pointed out that the Wisconsin primary was the following Tuesday and "it would look bad to quit after a defeat." Johnson asked him to draft a withdrawal statement like the one that had been prepared for the State of the Union message. On Sunday, March 31, there were animated discussions within the Johnson family about the wisdom of the decision, but the president remained firm in his determination to leave politics.

That evening a stunned nation heard Lyndon Johnson first announce that the bombing of North Vietnam would stop except in the area north of the demilitarized zone between North and South Vietnam. He also declared that he was designating Averell Harriman, a veteran diplomat, as his representative to any peace negotiations in which North Vietnam might wish to participate. He stressed American willingness to withdraw if North Vietnam allowed South Vietnam to live in peace. Finally, he reviewed his own public career and then announced, "I shall not seek, and I will not accept, the nomination of my party for another term as your President."

The reasons for Lyndon Johnson's withdrawal have been much debated since it was first announced. The initial impulse clearly related to Johnson's uncertain health. His wife had watched his physical condition deteriorate during the early months of 1968. She was an important voice reinforcing his inclination to drop out of politics.

The burdens of the presidency also weighed heavily on Johnson. He found the "goldfish bowl" of the office confining, and by 1967 he was a president almost imprisoned in the White House. Antiwar protesters nagged him at every public engagement, and the safest locations for speeches and appearances became military installations. A presidential campaign would have been an ordeal of protest and potential violence no matter how well guarded the president was.

Johnson also knew his political prospects were poor. Aides reassured him that he would win the Democratic nomination and the election. In fact, Johnson would have been pressed to gain the nomination and then to run successfully in the fall campaign. His poll ratings showed that more than 52 percent of Americans disliked his policies and 63 percent were against his handling of the war. His personality and his record would be the focus of Republican attacks. He might win in a three-man race against Nixon and George Wallace, but governing the country after the election would be difficult. In a two-man race with a Republican challenger, Johnson would have little support in the South and West, especially in California. He would also be in serious trouble in the agricultural Midwest. With the Democratic left disaffected, a victorious electoral coalition for Johnson would be difficult to assemble in 1968.

The nature of the battle he faced for the Democratic nomination contributed to Johnson's decision not to run. His hatred for Robert Kennedy was so profound that the prospect of losing the nomination to the New York senator was distasteful in the extreme. He later told a biographer, "The thing I feared from the first day of my Presidency was actually coming true. Robert Kennedy had openly announced his intention to reclaim the throne in the memory of his brother. And the American people, swayed by the magic of the name, were dancing in the streets. The whole situation was unbearable for me." Rather than face humiliation at Robert Kennedy's hands, Johnson stepped aside and frustrated his rival.

The decision followed a familiar pattern in Johnson's life. Before other campaigns he had often wavered about whether he should run. Usually friends or family stiffened his resolve to do what they knew he wanted to do. Lady Bird Johnson had played such a role in 1964 when her husband wavered before accepting the Democratic nomination. In 1968 no strong voice emerged among the people around Johnson to tell him that he should remain in politics. With their silence they confirmed Johnson's own judgment that his political career was ending.

The president's announcement shook the political landscape in 1968 and realigned the prospects of all the other candidates. The most immediate beneficiary of Johnson's decision seemed to be Robert Kennedy. Richard Nixon said the New York senator should now be favored to win the Democratic nomination. The Kennedy campaign phoned Democrats around the country urging them to enlist with the probable winner. Yet there was no stampede. During the period between his entry into the race and Johnson's withdrawal, Kennedy had waged a frenetic campaign to arouse popular support for his cause. He had spoken on college campuses to adoring audiences. His rhetoric had been intense. "In these next eight months," he said in Kansas, "we are going to decide what this country will stand for—and what kind of men we are." Since Kennedy lacked the support of Democratic organizations, he had to rely on popular enthusiasm. "I have to win through the people," he said. "Otherwise I am not going to win."

The tone of his speeches and the thrust of his campaign failed to impress the more moderate wing of the Democratic party. Kennedy had been a rough political operator during the campaign of 1960 and when he was attorney general. Resentments lingered from his earlier harsh style. The senator could still be abrupt in soliciting support. He called one Democratic woman in the hospital in mid-March and reminded her, "You wouldn't be in Washington if it hadn't been for us." The cumulative impact of Kennedy's emotional public campaign and hardball private tactics left many Democrats still looking for an alternative after Johnson withdrew from the race.

Senator McCarthy won an impressive victory in the Wisconsin primary on April 2. He beat the president easily with 56.2 percent of the vote to Johnson's 34.6 percent. Kennedy received a little more than 6 percent as a write-in candidate. Yet, with Johnson out of the race, the Wisconsin contest seemed an afterthought. It gave McCarthy no infusion of momentum.

Johnson's departure shifted the focus of the McCarthy race. He was an attractive protest candidate when the Democratic nominee was likely to be Lyndon Johnson and the chief issue the Vietnam War. With Johnson gone, the question arose of McCarthy's qualifications to be president and his strength as an anti–Robert Kennedy alternative. Even some of his own workers had reservations about McCarthy's capacity to be president. "Every week or two," said a campaign worker, "McCarthy would do or not do something which again brought into question his suitability for the presidency." McCarthy's advocacy of a less powerful presidency also caused some in his campaign and outside it to wonder whether he could meet the challenges of the office that went beyond the Vietnam War.

There was also the matter of McCarthy's commitment to civil rights. His record in the Senate was generally strong, but he lacked the passionate commitment to the cause that characterized Robert Kennedy's appeal that spring. Within the McCarthy campaign in Wisconsin, staff argued over making a strong appeal to black voters in Milwaukee. In the end they decided to add black workers to the campaign and make McCarthy more visible in ghetto areas. It was not clear how McCarthy would fare when he had to stand on his own merits against candidates more popular than Johnson.

Johnson's withdrawal opened the way for still another Democrat to enter the presidential race. Hubert Humphrey had not expected to have a chance for the White House in 1968 when the year opened. He anticipated another campaign as Johnson's running mate. After the events of March 31, however, Humphrey became the favorite of Democratic

moderates and conservatives. He had learned about the
president's decision that Sunday, and Johnson told him, "If
you're going to run, you'd better get ready damn quick."
Humphrey paused only briefly before he concluded that it
was his best remaining chance for the presidency. By the
time he returned to Washington from a trip to Mexico, he
was asking aides, "Has Bobby got it locked up yet?"

The fifty-seven-year-old Humphrey came to the presidential race with impressive credentials and formidable weaknesses. His strengths grew out of his record as a spokesman
for Democratic liberalism since his election to the Senate
from Minnesota in 1948. On civil rights, health care, and
other domestic issues, Humphrey had been in the vanguard
of those who had championed the aspirations of organized
labor, the poor, and black Americans. In foreign policy he
had stood for innovative ideas such as the Peace Corps and
limits on nuclear testing. He had been placed on the ticket
in 1964 because his record as a committed liberal would
reassure those with doubts about Johnson's own commitment
to reform.

Humphrey's years as vice president, however, had crippled his political standing among liberal Democrats. He had
been a loyal subordinate for Johnson, endorsing the policy on
Vietnam despite his own doubts about the wisdom of the
war. A man of enthusiasms, he had couched his defense of
the Vietnam involvement in glowing terms that left many
who heard him wondering if the vice president was a
sycophant for Johnson. Beyond that question, there were
Humphrey's limits as a campaigner. He could be an engross-
ing public speaker, but his energy often got the best of him
and he went on too long. Senators said he could speak a
hundred words a minute, with gusts up to two hundred
words.

In 1960 Humphrey had run against John F. Kennedy for the nomination. Kennedy's superior political skills and the abundant funds that the Kennedy family poured into the race, as well as some dirty tactics, had defeated him. The loss left its mark. Humphrey wondered now if he had a real chance to win, "or would I just be a punching bag for Kennedy, only to be humiliated and defeated in the Convention?" He had an equally vexing problem with Johnson. He would have to run close to the president's record but somehow establish himself as his own man. "If I run," he told a friend, "Johnson's not going to make it easy." Humphrey's inability to distance himself from the president would plague him throughout 1968.

Humphrey's candidacy faced another formidable obstacle at the outset. Because he was entering the race so late, it would be possible for him to qualify for only two of the spring primaries still to be held. To win the nomination he would have to gather delegates from those states that held caucuses and state conventions. There were more than enough delegates chosen in this way to give Humphrey the nomination; neither Kennedy nor McCarthy could win by running only in the primaries. This route meant, however, that Humphrey would be identified with the older style of Democratic politics and would owe any success to the party leaders and institutions that so many liberal Democrats scorned. Humphrey really had no choice, but his links with the "old politics" aroused resentments that troubled him until November.

One problem Humphrey did not have during the early weeks of his candidacy was money. As the candidate with the best chance to block Robert Kennedy, he became the beneficiary of all the forces within the Democratic party that sought to head off a Kennedy nomination. Big business, long

suspicious of Humphrey's liberalism, rallied to his campaign. Money from the Johnson presidential effort also
flowed toward him in April and May 1968. Organized labor
also strongly backed Humphrey. Because of Kennedy's attacks on corruption in organized labor during the 1950s and
while he was attorney general, many union leaders did not
wish to see him in the White House. Humphrey also
enjoyed significant support in the South among party leaders. A liberal outsider during the 1950s, he was now the
candidate of the Democratic establishment as he pursued the
1,231 delegates he needed for the party's nomination. He
announced his candidacy on April 27, 1968. An intense
struggle for control of the Democratic party lay ahead.

Johnson's withdrawal also brought about reassessments
within Republican ranks. For Richard Nixon, the president's
announcement offered him a fortuitous way to keep his
Vietnam policy vague and general. Until March 31, pressure
had been building on the Republican front-runner to be
more specific about his program for Southeast Asia. During
March he had indicated that he favored a greater reliance on
South Vietnamese troops to bear the brunt of the fighting.
Nonetheless, he was still less than specific about what he
would do once in office. His instincts were to remain as
quiet as possible on the issue. He told an aide, William
Safire, on March 24, "It would be better for me not to do
anything controversial for the time being. I don't want to get
into the crossfire between LBJ and Bobby—let them hit
each other, not me. But I don't like this 'secret plan'
business."

For a speech scheduled for March 31, Nixon's aides began
drafting a document that advocated greater use of airpower,
less emphasis on "search and destroy" missions aimed at
killing the enemy on the ground, and intensified diplomatic

pressure on the Soviet Union and China to bring about a negotiated settlement of the Vietnam War. In effect, Nixon reached the same conclusion as the Johnson administration: winning the war in Vietnam was not possible within the limits of the resources available to the United States. But Nixon did not have to set out his conclusions on March 31. When the White House asked the networks for time to carry the president's speech, Nixon canceled his address.

The day after the president's withdrawal announcement, Nixon declared he would make no further public statements about Vietnam and the war for several weeks while the president was carrying on his negotiations. In effect, the Republican leader could now avoid saying anything specific about his intentions. He also began a tacit political alliance with Lyndon Johnson that persisted throughout much of 1968 and had a significant effect on the outcome of the election.

By March 31 Nixon had also apparently staved off a challenge from his most serious Republican rival. After Nixon won in New Hampshire, moderate Republicans pressed Nelson Rockefeller publicly to enter the race. Rockefeller very much wanted to be president. Governor of New York since 1959, he believed his talents suited him for the White House. His race against Barry Goldwater in 1964, however, had left conservative Republicans permanently embittered against him. Rockefeller always looked better as a potential presidential candidate than he did once formally announced. He preferred to be selected rather than have to pursue the nomination. In early 1968 his soundings indicated that he would not succeed against Nixon. Rockefeller thus announced on March 21 that he would not be a candidate in 1968. In the process the New York governor embarrassed a key supporter. Governor Spiro Agnew of Maryland had organized a Draft Rockefeller Committee, and the announcement took him by surprise. Nixon soon made personal overtures to Agnew, and the two men found a common rapport that grew as the national convention neared.

The Republican nomination thus seemed to be safely in Nixon's grasp by April 1, 1968. He knew, however, that his real opposition might come from Ronald Reagan on the right of the party. The California governor was preserving his pose of noncandidacy while he waited to see if Nixon might falter. Reagan was already an impressive fund-raiser for party candidates, and he continued to be a drawing card on the Republican banquet circuit. Reagan's strategy was to be a favorite-son candidate from California, block Nixon's nomination on the first ballot, and thus inherit his Southern and Western support. But first Nixon would have to be stopped, and that eventuality seemed less and less likely as the spring of 1968 progressed.

Meanwhile, George Wallace was having growing success in placing his name on the ballot in every state. His standing in the polls rose slowly but perceptibly. He was the choice of 10 percent of the voters in one poll in October 1967. By March 1968 he had climbed to 15 percent of the vote in a three-way contest with Nixon and Johnson. One pollster concluded a few months later that "the strong possibility exists that third-party candidate George Wallace would deny either major party candidate the electoral votes needed to win."

Between the time of the Tet offensive and Johnson's departure from the presidential race, the issue of Vietnam dominated the public agenda. To that extent the election came to seem that it was about the American role in Southeast Asia rather than any domestic issue. That impression was misleading. Events following the speech of Lyndon

Johnson on March 31 demonstrated the extent to which other issues were animating the electorate. On April 4, 1968, Dr. Martin Luther King, Jr., was assassinated in Memphis, Tennessee. Across the nation blacks expressed their grief and anger in demonstrations and riots. The issue of race and the problem of "law and order" forced its way back into the presidential election of 1968. American society faced a time of turmoil and testing over an unpopular war and the question of racial justice.

3

The Violent Spring

DURING 1968 THE nation seemed to lurch from one shock to another. Four days after Lyndon Johnson's political abdication and two days after Eugene McCarthy won the Wisconsin primary, Dr. Martin Luther King, Jr., was killed at the Lorraine Motel where he was staying in Memphis, Tennessee. He was in Memphis to lend support to a strike of garbage workers. Reports of his assassination provoked rage and violence among blacks across the nation. In Washington, D.C., New York, Chicago, and other cities large and small, arson, violence, and looting erupted during the days that followed. "This is it, baby," said one black man in Washington. "The shit is going to hit the fan now. We ought to burn the place down right now." Ten people died in Washington, and more than seven hundred fires were set.

Politicians had focused on the war in Vietnam as the nation's major concern during the first three months of 1968. In a larger sense, the issue of race was a more salient domestic issue for Americans white and black at the end of the 1960s. The civil rights revolution, and the response that followed it, revealed tensions within the body politic over this most volatile of subjects. King's death laid bare the extent to which race still divided Americans during the presidency of Lyndon B. Johnson.

By 1968 the idealistic fervor for civil rights evident at the beginning of the decade had seriously diminished. An issue that had helped Democrats politically through 1964 now became an electoral liability. Fissures between blacks and whites had widened. In addition, blacks themselves were now divided about how best to pursue their agenda. For many blacks the achievements of the civil rights movement had not brought them close to economic or social equality with whites.

Initially, the civil rights campaigns of the early 1960s had commanded the support of most white Americans outside the South. In February 1964, for example, 72 percent of non-Southern whites told the Gallup poll that the Johnson administration was either "about right" or was not "fast enough" in its push for civil rights. The Civil Rights Act of 1964, which established legal equality in public accommodations and outlawed segregation in education and employment, and the Voting Rights Act of 1965, which struck down political barriers to black participation, seemed even-handed efforts to assure all citizens equal treatment before the law. For most Northern voters, segregation was at bottom a Southern problem. They did not expect that extending these legal rights to blacks would change the way race relations functioned outside of Dixie.

But problems arose after 1965 when the federal government enforced these new statutes. Carrying the provisions of the law into practice demanded bureaucratic decrees from Washington that addressed segregated school systems, discrimination in housing and employment, and the allocation of tax revenues. As these issues and policies moved outside the South to affect Northern voters in middle-class and lower-middle-class areas, support for the Democratic civil rights program dropped sharply. Voters saw it as a threat to property values, neighborhood integrity, and ethnic cohesion. As a labor union official wrote after Democratic defeats in the 1966 elections, "All over the country, civil rights is now equated with losing the savings invested in your home."

Equally devastating to Democrats was the emergence of urban violence as a black response to conditions in the nation's large cities. The riots in the Watts district of Los Angeles were not the first such disturbances. During 1964 there had been outbreaks of rioting in New York, Philadelphia, and Paterson, New Jersey. The Watts violence of 1965 received extensive television coverage of black youths engaged in looting and random destruction. Coming within days of the passage of the 1965 Voting Rights Act, the Watts riots indicated that legislation alone could not solve the racial issue.

During the "long, hot summers" of 1966, 1967, and 1968, ghetto riots became a fixture in the United States. Democrats faced the problem of explaining how their programs to deal with black grievances had evoked such a destructive response. Republicans charged that the Johnson administration was undermining social stability. "We have been talking a long time about color," said Senator Everett M. Dirksen, the Republican leader in the Senate, "when in fact we should also be talking about conduct." By August 1966 the Harris poll found that 70 percent of white Americans now believed that blacks were "trying to move too fast."

While white sentiment toward civil rights was cooling, opinion among blacks was moving in a contrasting direction.

The emphasis had shifted from a demand for legal equality to a more assertive call for equal economic and social conditions. A militant mood had appeared, especially among younger blacks who did not wish to wait for white America to grant them rights and privileges that should have been theirs all along. In the South such leaders as Stokely Carmichael of the Student Nonviolent Coordinating Committee had galvanized his audiences in 1966 with strong language. "We been saying freedom for six years—and we ain't got nothin'. What we gonna start saying now is 'Black Power!'" The black civil rights movement broke apart over the issue of Black Power. Those who believed in the need for coalitions with whites confronted those, such as Carmichael, who urged blacks to use their own resources in the struggle.

The most visible victim of this process was Martin Luther King. He had become a national figure during the 1950s when he first led the boycott of blacks against the system of segregated buses in Montgomery, Alabama. King preached a gospel of nonviolence based on the teachings of Henry Thoreau and Mohandas Ghandi. Soon he was the apparent embodiment of the civil rights struggle and its most eloquent champion. His speech during the March on Washington in 1963, with its moving cadences of "I have a dream," touched the national conscience. His demonstrations in Selma, Alabama, and elsewhere laid the groundwork for passage of the Civil Rights Act of 1964 and the Voting Rights Act of 1965. To many whites King seemed a responsible black spokesman working for constructive policies.

As other blacks moved to a more militant position, King experienced the more subtle racism of the North in campaigns to integrate housing in Chicago. He also became critical of the war in Vietnam. "In a real sense," he said in April 1967, "the Great Society has been shot down on the battlefields of Vietnam." King's attack on Johnson's war policies separated him from the White House. He moved closer to embracing socialism as a way to redistribute the wealth of the nation. He promised to unite the peace movement and the civil rights movement "until the *very foundations of our nation are shaken.*" No matter what King did, he could not satisfy young blacks who wanted a revolution in the United States, but his language angered the administration and mainstream black leaders who had access to politicians and power. By the time Johnson withdrew from the presidential race, King's career was in crisis. A few weeks before he was murdered, he was discussing more aggressive tactics of nonviolence and social disruption to end the war and achieve rights for black Americans.

The riots that broke out when King was killed soon led to congressional action on an open-housing law that had been stalled in Congress. Republicans supported the bill in part to avoid a stronger law and, at Richard Nixon's request, to remove the issue from the forthcoming campaign. The law represented a symbolic response of white America to what had happened in the wake of King's death. The other reaction of whites, however, was more ominous in both political and social terms. Chicago's Mayor Richard J. Daley had ordered his police to "shoot to kill" rioters in that city. Political candidates soon began to emphasize law-and-order appeals in their speeches. Richard Nixon took readily to such a theme, and in his campaign appearances during the spring he declared, to appreciative applause, "Some of our courts have gone too far in weakening the peace forces as against the criminal forces, and we must restore the balance."

Nixon carefully framed his appeals for law and order in language that prevented opponents from accusing him of racial demagoguery. Such considerations did not trouble the candidate outside the existing party system whose ability to tap the racial fears of white Americans was making him a significant element in presidential politics, Governor George C. Wallace of Alabama.

Wallace told a Washington press conference on February 8, 1968, that he intended to enter the presidential race. "The bureaucrats and rhetoricians in Washington" should let "people in Ohio and New York and California decide themselves...what type of school system they are going to have," said Wallace's campaign literature. Politicians and reporters persistently underrated Wallace's prospects as his candidacy got under way. Democrats preferred not to face the implications of his appeal to Northern white voters. Republicans were equally anxious to avoid considering what Wallace did to their growing appeal to Southern whites. With Wallace in a three-candidate race, Republicans and Democrats were essentially deadlocked. Polls indicated that Wallace would win about 10 percent of the vote in a three-candidate race, and his total was creeping up during the spring of 1968.

By the time he took to the campaign trail, Wallace had become adept at tapping into the resentment that his supporters felt about the direction in which society was moving. He made no overtly racist appeals. "I am not against anybody because of color," he said. "I never have been." Instead he charged, "The Communist movement has been behind the civil rights movement." When he said that "it was never intended for the Federal Government to run the policies of local schools," his cheering audiences knew he was talking about desegregation and civil rights. "Integration is a matter to be decided by each State," he contended. "The States must determine if they feel it is of benefit to both races."

Wallace delivered these messages with practiced skill. His rallies had the flavor of a Country and Western stage show, a religious revival, and a political camp meeting. His standard lines drew thunderous applause. If he faced demonstrators as president, he knew how he would handle them. "When we get to be President, and some anarchist lies down in front of our car, it'll be the *last* car he'll ever lie down in front of." He tried to find the common bond of resentment among white voters North and South. "People always say that George Wallace just appeals to the crackers, the peckerwoods, and the rednecks," Wallace would say. As the crowd waited for the punch line, he added, "Well, George Wallace says there's an awful lot of us rednecks in this country—*and they're not all in the South!*" When he denounced liberals and bureaucrats, his listeners shouted their agreement.

Wallace formally announced his candidacy on April 1. His campaign was well financed, and his organization had placed his name on the ballot in all fifty states. Knowing he could not be elected president himself, Wallace hoped to hold the balance of power in a deadlocked election. He "would have the power to say just who *would* be the next President. And I make no secret that I would want something in return before I make my choice."

The social resentments that propelled Wallace to national prominence formed the context for the campaigns of the major party candidates during the spring of 1968. For

Richard Nixon, Wallace posed a clear threat to his electoral chances once Nixon had received the Republican nomination. During April little disturbed the smooth progress of the Nixon campaign. He easily defeated Ronald Reagan in the Wisconsin primary, where the California governor's name was on the ballot but he did not campaign. As the month ended, however, reports circulated that Nelson Rockefeller was reconsidering his earlier decision not to seek the presidency.

Urged on by Lyndon Johnson in secret and in public by major business leaders, Rockefeller announced on April 30 that he was back in the race. Since it was unlikely he could defeat Nixon in Republican primaries, Rockefeller needed to show he was electable where Nixon, a two-time loser, was not. Public opinion polls would do that, Rockefeller and his men believed. Then the victory-hungry Republicans would abandon Nixon for a proven winner. It was an ill-conceived approach. Rank-and-file Republicans across the nation hated Rockefeller as a man who had opposed Barry Goldwater in 1964, symbolized big government in New York State, and was trying to buy the GOP nomination. Even if the poll results ran Rockefeller's way, many Republicans would never turn to his candidacy. "If the polls show you well ahead of Nixon, that's going to make you even less popular" with Republicans, an aide told Rockefeller accurately.

Rockefeller spent a great deal of money during May and June, won the Massachusetts primary on the day he announced, and saw the polls move marginally in his favor. Surveys did not show, however, that Nixon would lose in the fall. In fact, in the Indiana, Nebraska, and Oregon primaries, Nixon won impressive victories over both Rockefeller and Reagan when their names appeared on the ballot. Clearly the average Republican voter wanted Nixon as the party's presidential candidate more than Rockefeller. Whether they would feel the same way in a Reagan-Nixon confrontation remained to be seen. For the moment, however, Rockefeller's entry into the Republican race had fallen flat. As June began his candidacy was lifeless.

Nixon continued to build his campaign appeal on the basis of voter uneasiness with the way the nation was moving on domestic issues. He tried out themes that would serve him well in the fall and that became lasting features of Republican campaigns into the future. What the country needed, he said on May 16, was a "new alignment for American unity" that would produce "a significant breakthrough toward what America needs: peaceful, orderly progress." For the first time he began talking about "the silent center, the millions of people in the middle of the political spectrum who do not demonstrate, who do not picket or protest loudly." His campaign literature proclaimed that "there is no cause that justifies rule by mob instead of by reason." He found in the nation "a rebellion against taxes, and against the ever-higher piling of Federal tax on state tax on local tax."

Wooing the South for its electoral votes and to stave off any challenge from Reagan, Nixon courted Senator John Tower of Texas and Senator Strom Thurmond of South Carolina. Thurmond was especially central to Nixon's chances; he had been the candidate of the States' Rights party in 1948 and was "the only Southern leader in the GOP who could rally Southerners to a Republican banner." At a meeting in Atlanta on May 31, Nixon assured Thurmond and other Southern Republicans that he would name conservatives to the Supreme Court, oppose "busing as a means of achieving racial balance in schools," and increase defense spending. The defense issue was particularly important to Thurmond. The South Carolina senator announced his support for Nixon a few days later when he said that the republican front-runner "offers the best hope of recovering from domestic lawlessness; a bloody no-win war in Southeast Asia; runaway spending and rising costs of living; strategic military inferiority; loss of influence in world affairs; and a power-grasping Supreme Court." Thurmond would prove to be the key to Nixon's convention success with Southern delegates.

While Republicans remained relatively unified during the spring, and Nixon's bandwagon continued to roll along without serious public opposition, the Democrats' situation did not improve after Johnson's withdrawal and the murder of Martin Luther King, Jr. Each one of the major candidates—Kennedy, McCarthy, and Humphrey—pursued the nomination energetically in April and May. In the process, whatever remained of intraparty unity vanished in a series of acrimonious primary and convention battles. Personality clashes and ideological disputes overshadowed electoral considerations and any kind of rational judgment about what was needed to beat the Republicans in the fall campaign. Still believing they were the normal majority party, Democrats did not adjust easily or effectively to the presence of a competitive Republican party and the third-party challenge of George Wallace.

In the wake of Johnson's withdrawal, the conventional wisdom in the press was that Robert Kennedy had become the front-runner for the nomination. Such a judgment rested on a faith in the Kennedy mystique among the American people and the presumed efficiency of the Kennedys as political operators. It took less account of Kennedy's specific problems as a national candidate for president. Despite his celebrity status, the New York senator was not as formidable in electoral terms as people at the time and later historians have believed. In May 1968, for example, he trailed Nixon by ten percentage points in the polls.

In any case, neither Eugene McCarthy nor Hubert Humphrey was prepared to step aside and concede the Democratic nomination to Robert Kennedy. McCarthy told aides, "It's narrowed down to Bobby and me." He intended to make Kennedy campaign against his own legacy. "We'll make him run against Jack ... and I'm Jack." In the absence of Lyndon Johnson, however, McCarthy's campaign lacked a clear public rationale. His supporters were a diverse mixture of radical Democrats who found even Robert Kennedy too conservative for their tastes, and liberals who looked back longingly to the articulate messages of Adlai Stevenson. For black and working-class audiences, McCarthy had little to offer. He seemed out of step with the black and Hispanic Democrats with whom Kennedy naturally communicated.

McCarthy's campaign reflected the ambivalence of its candidate. It was poorly organized, and McCarthy was not disposed to give his workers clear direction and purpose. "He seemed to pay no attention at all to his campaign," recalled one operative. "He viewed it as a spontaneous happening which he should not try to control." The presidential candidate was easily distracted, disliked emotional appeals, and sometimes seemed above all the excitement of the campaign. Some Democrats responded to his cool aloofness, others found his detachment infuriating. In the spring of 1968 his sudden rise to prominence gave him an untested electoral appeal that made him a difficult opponent for both Kennedy and Hubert Humphrey.

After rallying support from party regulars during April, and lining up funds to sustain his campaign, Vice President Humphrey prepared to announce his candidacy on April 27. In terms of national electoral appeal, he was the strongest of the three Democratic front-runners in 1968. As Northern liberals, Kennedy, McCarthy, and Humphrey all had modest support in the South and border states. Except for the Pacific Coast, they were also weak in the West. McCarthy ran well in the suburbs but not in the inner cities. Kennedy could capture the black voters in the cities and some of the disaffected white ethnic voters. Humphrey had residual support in each of these constituencies. One key to Humphrey's strength with party regulars was their sense that he would do the least electoral damage to local Democrats in the fall campaign.

Humphrey approached his announcement with typical ebullience. "Here we are," he told his audience, "the way politics ought to be in America, the politics of happiness, the politics of purpose, the politics of joy. And that's the way it's going to be, all the way, from here on in." The phrase "the politics of joy" struck a discordant note among many liberals who regarded it as further evidence of how out of touch with events Humphrey had become as part of the Johnson administration. Nonetheless, Humphrey began running strongly in the states where he needed to do well. During late April and into May he won a strong majority of delegates in such states as Maryland and Pennsylvania. Humphrey headquarters predicted he would be nominated on the first ballot; polls indi-

cated he was the choice among rank-and-file Democratic
voters.

Humphrey's lead emerged not because of any inherent
strength of his campaign organization. To appeal to the
younger voters who seemed so crucial in 1968, he named
Senators Fred Harris of Oklahoma and Walter Mondale of
Minnesota to run his campaign, United Democrats for
Humphrey. A number of people played significant roles,
including his vice-presidential aides, old political friends
from Minnesota, and longtime Democratic friends. The
result was an organization of confused and shifting align-
ments which confirmed the Washington perception that
Humphrey was not a good administrator. Still, the candidate's main problem remained his relationship with Lyndon
Johnson and Humphrey's need to establish his own political
identity.

While Humphrey moved toward a nomination based on
delegates obtained in the convention states, between early
May and early June, McCarthy and Kennedy waged a series
of bitter primary battles in Indiana, Nebraska, Oregon,
and California. The press concentrated on this exciting horse
race between two famous Democrats to see who would
become the most credible alternative to the vice president. Democratic liberalism indulged in a fratricidal display
which further contributed to the electoral problems of the
party in 1968 and beyond.

The McCarthy-Kennedy battles occurred as American
society watched with dismay further evidence of upheaval
among the younger generation on college campuses. The
most famous and visible of these confrontations occurred at
Columbia University in New York City. Located on Morningside Heights above the black district of Harlem, Columbia had long had a tense relationship with its neighbors. In

1968 these pressures focused on the university's plans to construct a new gymnasium in Morningside Park. While part of the proposed facility would be available for the use of local residents, most of the gym would serve the predominantly white and affluent student body of Columbia. At a time when students nationally were protesting the insensitivity of research universities to social needs and their willingness to collaborate with the established order, the Columbia gym issue aroused animosities among the university's small black student population. Radical students at Columbia distrusted the university's position on the draft and were looking for an occasion to dramatize their grievances. The gymnasium issue thus served as an excuse for radical Columbia students to publicize their marginal position within higher education.

Protests against the gymnasium and the Vietnam War at Columbia on April 23, 1968, led to a student occupation of the main building at the university. Within a few days five more buildings were seized. The students demanded that the gymnasium not be built and that the university recognize the Vietnam War was wrong. They also wanted amnesty for their actions. Negotiations failed to produce a settlement. Instead, on April 30 the New York City police evicted the occupying students. More than 500 students were arrested and 148 people injured, including 20 police. Three weeks later another occupation occurred, with another equally violent confrontation. This time more than 175 people were arrested and 68 were injured.

The events on Morningside Heights were another indication to American voters of a rapidly unraveling social fabric. Turmoil on campuses, like urban rioting, aroused fears about the stability of law and order in the nation. Richard Nixon called the events at Columbia "the first major skirmish in a revolutionary struggle to seize the universities of this country and transform them into sanctuaries for radicals and vehicles for revolutionary politics and social goals." Since the language of the Columbia protesters resembled what Democratic contenders were saying on the campaign trail—about the Vietnam War, racism, and the failure of the older generation, for example—voters blamed the party for fostering campus unrest.

The confrontation between Eugene McCarthy and Robert Kennedy began with the Indiana primary on May 7. It was not a state likely to be carried by any Democratic candidate in 1968. Indiana had voted for the Democratic presidential choice only twice, in 1936 and 1964, and Nixon was favored to win easily in the general election. Wallace sentiment was strong in the southern part of the state, and racial tensions were evident in the industrialized north with a substantial black population. The Democratic party organization, led by Governor Roger D. Branigan, was hostile to both liberal candidates, especially Kennedy. The Democratic primary became a three-man race, with Branigan as the favorite-son candidate of the regulars who had supported Johnson and now preferred Humphrey. Still, Kennedy and his aides decided that Indiana offered the best opportunity to knock McCarthy out of the race quickly and make the search for delegates a choice between Humphrey and Kennedy. When Kennedy went in, McCarthy did so as well.

Kennedy and his family poured several million dollars into the primary, blanketing the state with radio and television commercials, billboards, and literature. The goal was to assemble a coalition of the state's black voters and white ethnic working-class Democrats who had admired John Kennedy. In the highly conservative climate of Indiana in the spring of 1968, Kennedy also emphasized more than he had in the past his law-and-order credentials as a former attorney general who had been "for three-and-a-half years, chief law enforcement officer of the United States." He cut his hair, muted his speaking style, and played down his similarities to his late brother. These changes were designed to soften Kennedy's perceived image as "a too-aggressive opportunist running on John Kennedy's reputation, with too much of an appeal to the very young and immature."

In Indiana, where antiwar protests were unpopular, Kennedy changed his stance on the Vietnam War. Placing less emphasis on a negotiated settlement of the conflict, he argued for improving U.S. military and diplomatic prospects. He talked of the role businessmen could play in addressing the problems of the cities, including tax credits for firms that helped to develop the inner city. These statements were necessary concessions to conservative sentiments in Indiana, but they illustrated Democratic problems in 1968 in appealing to the broad electorate. Republicans could always make a stronger case for the same policies.

Eugene McCarthy's campaign did not go well in Indiana. Johnson's withdrawal had left McCarthy's student canvassers without the war issue to stress to the voters. As a result, the impact of young people was not as positive as it had been in New Hampshire. Within the campaign organization itself, discord prevailed as local McCarthy supporters fought with members of his national leadership. There were mix-ups in speaking schedules; campaign literature was not available;

and the focus of the canvass was on sparsely populated rural Indiana. "At times we were ready to shoot ourselves," said one McCarthy worker.

McCarthy's residual appeal remained intact. For Democrats who disliked Johnson and Kennedy in equal measure, the senator from Minnesota seemed a calm, rational alternative. The enthusiastic crowds that surrounded Kennedy made other voters fearful. McCarthy played on these apprehensions with his calls for "your patience, your attention" as he offered "a politics of participation and a politics of personal response on the part of the citizens of this country." There was also a good deal of innovation in some of McCarthy's themes. He argued, "The Cold War in Europe is over. There's no need to go on fighting it." As he had before, he called for the ouster of J. Edgar Hoover, director of the Federal Bureau of Investigation, and the replacement of Secretary of State Dean Rusk. Attacks on these established figures pleased McCarthy's liberal adherents but did little to reassure Indiana voters about the candidate's concern for the economic and social issues of inflation and crime.

When the votes were tallied on May 7, Kennedy led the field in Indiana. He received 42.3 percent of the total, or 328,118 votes, to Branigan's 30.7 percent, and 27 percent (209,965 votes) for McCarthy. The outcome satisfied neither McCarthy nor Kennedy. For Kennedy the victory was not so decisive that it would drive McCarthy from the field. In fact, since McCarthy had done slightly better than expected, the Minnesota senator believed the primary was a positive for him. "We have tested the enemy," he said. "We know his techniques, we know his weaknesses."

Kennedy won the black vote easily but also did well in

blue-collar districts where Wallace had shown strength. From these facts observers at the time and scholars since have concluded that Kennedy's showing in Indiana indicated that he might be able to achieve a working coalition of whites and blacks and heal some of the rifts among Democrats. That conclusion exaggerates the significance of Kennedy's Indiana vote. In the Republican primary, Nixon polled 508,000 votes, more than any one of the Democratic contenders, and he won more than a million votes when he carried the state against Humphrey and Wallace in the fall. Kennedy's coalition represented more the hard core of the Democratic base in Indiana than a potential nucleus of a winning majority in a general election.

While Kennedy and McCarthy fought in Indiana, Humphrey continued to amass convention delegates with regularity. His confident managers, Senators Mondale and Harris, talked of a first-ballot victory. Meanwhile, the primary race moved on to the Western plains in the Nebraska election of May 14. From the outset, the McCarthy effort in Nebraska was minimal. The main emphasis of his campaign was directed toward the next primary in the more friendly state of Oregon, and the resources committed to Nebraska were limited. For Kennedy, on the other hand, Nebraska was an attractive race. The farm policies of the Johnson administration were unpopular with Nebraska Democrats, and Kennedy began the race with a double-digit lead over McCarthy in the polls.

Nebraska was a strongly Republican state which had voted overwhelmingly for Nixon against John Kennedy in 1960. Fewer than 200,000 Democratic voters had to be reached, and the Kennedy organization could use its resources for phone banks and campaign workers to blanket the state. While Kennedy's appearances in Nebraska were highly successful, McCarthy seemed uninterested and more concerned about the next contest in Oregon. The result was an impressive Kennedy victory on May 14. He won almost 52 percent of the vote to McCarthy's 32 percent. The Kennedy forces immediately sought to dismiss McCarthy as a serious alternative to their man. He was, said one Kennedy aide, no longer "a credible candidate."

Such talk did not impress McCarthy, who sensed that Oregon would be friendlier territory for the kind of campaign he was making. "We are going on to Oregon," he told supporters after the Nebraska vote. The Oregon primary, held a week before the California vote, would be a significant test going into the most important primary of the year in California. The result in Nebraska indicated that Kennedy appealed to the base of Democratic support, as he had shown in Indiana. But there was little chance he or any Democrat could carry Nebraska in the fall. Nixon won the state overwhelmingly six months later.

McCarthy's campaign, battered after two consecutive primary defeats, revived in the more favorable atmosphere of Oregon. Long opposed to the Vietnam War, Democrats in the state responded positively to McCarthy's early denunciations of the Asian conflict. In a state with few minorities and a relative absence of serious urban problems, Kennedy's concern with the nation's social ills seemed irrelevant. Organized labor disliked Kennedy because of his role in opposing the Teamsters Union in the 1950s. For McCarthy the rural state with small towns and cities was well-suited to his low-key rhetoric and Minnesota farm background. The McCarthy forces in Oregon were well organized, and in this instance the Kennedy campaign suffered because of its dependence on the help of Congresswoman Edith Green. (The Kennedy forces believed her to be more powerful than she really was.) Early polls showed McCarthy running even with Kennedy. A sizable pro-Johnson vote remained among party conservatives, and it was likely to turn to McCarthy in the polling booths. During a speech in California in mid-May, Kennedy said, "I think that if I get beaten in any primary, I am not a very viable candidate." His comment raised the stakes of the Oregon primary.

By the time of the Oregon race, tensions between Kennedy and McCarthy had intensified. During earlier races, supporters of Kennedy had circulated leaflets attacking McCarthy for his Senate votes against a minimum-wage law in 1960 and against a provision of the 1965 Voting Rights Act to repeal the poll tax in the South. McCarthy's camp responded with charges that Kennedy had engaged in illegal wiretapping during his service as attorney general, including the telephone of Martin Luther King, Jr. These nasty exchanges probably influenced few Democratic voters. As Kennedy conceded, the people who voted for McCarthy would have done so even if he had voted wrong on issues consistently. They were that bitter. The emotional temperature of the strife among Democrats was rising, reducing the chances for reestablishing party unity for the general election.

In Oregon McCarthy sharpened his attacks on the Vietnam War and the links between war policies that spanned the Kennedy and Johnson administrations. That approach hit Robert Kennedy at a vulnerable point, for the New York senator was now attacking policies with which his dead brother had been identified. "Involvement in Vietnam was no accident," McCarthy said, "it did not happen overnight." There was continuity in how Americans had conducted their foreign affairs, McCarthy charged, for which Robert Kennedy needed to answer. "Any man who played a prominent role in developing the policies of the early sixties, I think, can be called upon to explain his role in those policies, and not just in those policies but in the development of the process." McCarthy indicated he would not under any circumstances reach an accommodation with Kennedy.

Kennedy never found his stride in Oregon. His high-intensity campaigning style put voters off, and, as defeat neared, his heightened efforts compounded his problems. An aide observed that Oregon "is all one great white middle-class suburb" whose voters Kennedy "frightened." With the United States moving toward a politics in which these suburbs would hold increasing electoral power, Kennedy's difficulties in Oregon suggest that his national coalition-building powers had inherent limits.

McCarthy defeated Kennedy in Oregon on May 28. The Minnesota senator received 45 percent of the vote to 39 percent for Kennedy; the remainder was scattered among Johnson, Humphrey, and write-in ballots. At the McCarthy victory celebration the crowd chanted, "Gene in '68, Bobby'll have to wait." McCarthy told them, "Here we had the right issues and the right candidate, and here it was just a question of finding our constituency." Kennedy congratulated McCarthy and accepted his family's first electoral defeat with public grace. As it turned out, the Oregon results did not help McCarthy. Kennedy's defeat helped Humphrey's chances for a nomination and thus worked against McCarthy's long-range aspirations for the presidency. And the bitterness now generated between the McCarthy and Kennedy camps proved an important element in the continuing factional warfare that plagued the Democrats throughout 1968.

Kennedy's chances for the nomination now hinged on victory in California. If he failed to win that large bloc of delegates, he would have no chance to convince wavering Democrats in the East to leave Humphrey and support his candidacy. Should he lose in California, the delegates already committed to him would jump on the Humphrey bandwagon overnight. McCarthy, on the other hand, needed a win over Kennedy to emerge as the anti-Humphrey alternative—though some of his staff members thought a narrow loss would be best. That would keep Kennedy and McCarthy evenly balanced as opponents of Humphrey and increase the possibility of a deadlocked national convention. In either event, McCarthy had to campaign vigorously in California if he wished to make a respectable showing against Kennedy.

In terms of organization and money, the primary contest in California was now one of relative equals. The long-standing antiwar sentiment in the state provided a grass-roots base for the McCarthy campaign. His triumph in Oregon brought in fresh contributions which enabled his campaign to purchase the huge amounts of television and radio advertising needed to cover California's large population. The candidate himself was more involved in the race than in previous primaries, and that added energy to his campaign in California between May 29 and June 4.

Kennedy's campaign was equally well organized and efficient, with a network of one hundred campaign head-quarters across the state, an abundance of volunteers, and ample funds for media messages. The candidate's most secure base was among black and Hispanic voters. Kennedy

appeared in minority precincts to overwhelming public ado-
ration. Tens of thousands of people would surge toward his
car, trying to touch him or shake his hand. Among white
voters in the California suburbs, however, sentiment was
split between Kennedy and McCarthy. McCarthy was running strongly among Democrats who had voted for Adlai
Stevenson in the 1950s.

Until California, Kennedy had refused to stage a public
debate with McCarthy. After the Oregon result Kennedy
could no longer use his perceived front-runner status to
avoid a confrontation with his rival. The two men appeared
on a television broadcast on June 1 for their first face-to-face
encounter of the campaign. Neither prepared diligently for
the debate. The McCarthy camp was confident its man
would easily win; Kennedy held briefings but seemed distracted.

The debate itself had some heated moments. When asked
what they would do about Vietnam, McCarthy indicated
that a coalition government, including some communists,
was necessary to bring the war to an end. Kennedy challenged that position on the grounds that it would involve
"forcing a coalition on the government of Saigon." As he
had done in Indiana, Kennedy was careful not to repudiate
the war. McCarthy responded that he would accept such a
coalition but would not impose one on the South Vietnamese.

In a key exchange on the issue of the cities and the
problems of race, Kennedy suggested that the government
invest in the rehabilitation of ghetto areas. It would be
better, McCarthy offered, to relocate some ghetto residents
in areas outside the inner city. Kennedy replied that such
a strategy might produce "catastrophic" results, and he

added the inflammatory remark, "You say you are going to take ten thousand black people and move them into Orange County" (a conservative suburb near Los Angeles). There were further discussions of Kennedy's responsibility for the policies and failures of his brother's administration.

Going into the debate, the conventional wisdom had been that McCarthy was the superior performer who would handle the less adept Kennedy. When the two men battled on even terms for most of the program, Kennedy exceeded the press's expectations. In the reaction to the debate, newspaper polls put Kennedy ahead of his rival. "It was clear," said one McCarthy speech writer, "that Kennedy could take McCarthy head-on, with no fear of his magic powers." Whether it was boredom on McCarthy's part or a fear of showing more eagerness for the nomination than he believed a candidate should, McCarthy missed a chance to establish an evident superiority over his rival. The debate took much of the steam out of McCarthy's campaign workers.

The results on June 4 gave Kennedy a victory in the California primary—clear, but not as decisive as his supporters had hoped for. He gathered 46.4 percent of the vote to 41.8 percent for McCarthy. A slate of former Johnson supporters won about 12 percent. At the same time Kennedy won a strong victory in the South Dakota primary, where he had 50 percent of the vote to 20 percent for McCarthy. Delegates pledged to Johnson and Hubert Humphrey gained 30 percent of the vote in the state. That election night Kennedy hoped he might now persuade the McCarthy supporters "that I'm the only candidate against the war that can beat Humphrey." He added, "My only chance is to chase Hubert's ass all over the country."

Robert Kennedy, of course, never got the chance to implement that strategy. He made a victory statement in the Embassy Ballroom at the Ambassador Hotel in Los Angeles shortly after midnight on June 5, 1968. He pledged to heal the divisions within the country, "whether it's between blacks and whites, between the poor and the more affluent, or between age groups or on the war in Vietnam," so that the nation "can start to work together." Leaving the ballroom, he was passing through a hotel kitchen when he was fatally wounded by an assassin, Sirhan Sirhan. Robert Kennedy died early on the morning of June 6 from the effects of the gunshot wounds he had received.

The days that followed were filled with memorable scenes as Kennedy's body was carried to New York for a requiem mass and then taken by train to Washington, D.C., for burial at Arlington Cemetery. Thousands of people lined the route of the train, and two women were killed when they spilled onto the track in the way of trains going in the other direction. Politicians adjourned the campaign momentarily, and the press explored the phenomenon of growing social violence in the United States. The death of Robert Kennedy came to symbolize the anguish of a year when shock followed shock in bewildering succession.

Robert Kennedy's death in the middle of the campaign left unanswered forever the question of whether he could have defeated Hubert Humphrey for the Democratic nomination. Friends of the senator later claimed he had a good chance, arguing that Humphrey's delegate strength, while impressive on paper, was soft. "Humphrey had a lot of delegates," said one McCarthy backer, "but not enough to win." According to this view, a determined Kennedy, campaigning energetically, could have swayed wavering Humphrey support and united with McCarthy backers to win the nomination.

In the years after Kennedy's death, a related argument arose: only he among the Democratic candidates in 1968 could have rebuilt the coalition of white ethnic voters and blacks that had won for John Kennedy in 1960. In this scenario, Robert Kennedy could have reached across barriers of class and race to unify disadvantaged whites and disaffected minorities and staved off the Republican dominance of the 1970s and 1980s. This romantic vision especially appealed to liberal Democrats in the years when their fortunes in electoral politics were bleak.

No one can say for sure what would have happened had Kennedy lived, but the evidence suggests that his unifying abilities would have been inadequate to the task that confronted the Democrats in 1968. Despite his enthusiastic crowds, Kennedy lacked popularity with the broad mass of voters. In much of the South, animosity toward him was intense. Had he won the Democratic nomination, it is hard, for example, to visualize him winning the state of Texas. Humphrey did so in the fall, in part because of George Wallace and also because Lyndon Johnson and John Connally pulled the warring Texas Democrats together for their party's candidate. It is inconceivable that such efforts would have been made on behalf of the presidential candidacy of Robert Kennedy. Kennedy's advocates use his success at winning a plurality of Democratic voters as proof that he would have been a strong national candidate in the fall election. More likely, he would not have run as well as Humphrey did in November 1968.

After Kennedy's death the lineup for the fall elections seemed assured. Nixon was well in front for the Republican nomination, Humphrey would win when the Democrats met in Chicago in late August, and the Wallace third-party candidacy would be in the field as an unknown and potentially powerful element. Beneath the surface, however, all was not as secure as it seemed. Humphrey had the problems of Lyndon Johnson and Vietnam to address if he was to be a successful candidate. Richard Nixon faced a potential challenge from the popular Ronald Reagan. Finally, George Wallace had to show that he was more than a wasted third-party vote. The summer of 1968 proved as volatile and complex as the violent spring.

4

Nixon's the One

THE MURDER OF Robert Kennedy had no serious impact on the campaigns of George Wallace or Richard Nixon. But it left the Democrats' situation in continuing turmoil. The party seemed unable to find a secure place from which to prepare for the fall contest against the Republicans. Kennedy's passing disrupted both his major rivals.

For Eugene McCarthy, the personal effects of the assassination were the most devastating. His candidacy never recovered from the shock of what happened in Los Angeles. He said later that his goal "after the primaries" was to create "sufficient strength" to ensure that the Vietnam issue received a full airing at the Democratic National Convention. He hoped in the end to induce Humphrey to break with Lyndon Johnson over the war. McCarthy seems to have recognized in early June that he probably could not deny the vice president the nomination.

McCarthy's personal course during the summer of 1968 helped to assure Humphrey's selection, but it also limited the ability of antiwar Democrats to influence the convention. For McCarthy to have a powerful impact on the delegates, he needed to keep his own candidacy viable. Instead the Minnesota senator "withdrew" as a committed participant in the nomination process. Nothing formal was ever said, but, as one of his speech writers noted bitterly, "Gene McCarthy regressed to his balanced presentation of self, to the sacred ceremony of his personality."

During the weeks of June and July McCarthy distanced himself from his campaign and the exuberant supporters who still yearned to go all out for him. He made no positive overtures to the former supporters of Robert Kennedy. He refused to court governors and other Democratic leaders who might have come out for him against Humphrey. He ruled out efforts to woo wavering Humphrey delegates, either in behind-the-scenes negotiations or through public speeches against Humphrey's candidacy. The senator also refused to go into the cities and appeal to black voters who had been so strong for Robert Kennedy. McCarthy complained that the presidential nominating process was endless and unrewarding: "It's as if someone gave you the football and you're running with it, but the field never ends."

A few positive moments indicated the residual power of McCarthy's appeal. On June 18 the McCarthy forces won the Democratic primary in New York and received sixty-two delegate votes. Victory in that state required extensive grassroots organizing because of a complicated selection process mandated by the New York party. It was a testament to the enthusiasm that liberal, antiwar Democrats still brought to McCarthy's cause. Elsewhere, Humphrey's dominance of the party machinery produced victories for the vice president in the Connecticut, Montana, and Minnesota conventions. Similar results occurred in Kentucky, Texas, and Washington. McCarthy's supporters began to focus on the way the Democratic nominating system, using a "unit rule" which ceded all votes in a delegation to the majority, denied representation to a defeated minority.

Some of these complaints were self-serving. In those states where McCarthy's people won control, they had no qualms about giving their man all the available votes. In local conventions in Minnesota, for example, longtime Democratic leaders found themselves stripped of their power. Nonetheless, the newcomers to politics who were most of McCarthy's following were outraged at party rules that allowed Humphrey's campaign to use such tactics against their candidate.

Kennedy's death shook Hubert Humphrey as well, and he failed to make good use of the months of June, July, and August to strengthen his campaign organization and to find workable themes for the fall election. One of the vice president's abiding concerns was money for his campaign. Once Kennedy died, the large contributors who had supported Humphrey so generously in April and May returned to their normal Republican allegiance. In late June, for example, the Humphrey campaign trimmed fifty campaign workers from its payroll to save money. A month later the fall advertising strategy fell behind schedule because the campaign had failed to make an initial payment to its New York advertising agency.

Once Humphrey became the clear front-runner, he also became a lightning rod for demonstrations and heckling from the more virulent antiwar groups. The cry became "Dump the Hump," and signs linked Humphrey with Johnson: "Why Change the Ventriloquist for the Dummy?" Other protesters told the vice president, "Wash the blood off your hands." Humphrey's responses to these attacks, while spirited at times, lacked the edge that Wallace imparted to his replies to heckling. As one of Humphrey's aides recalled, the vice president "became associated in the American mind with unruliness, loud demonstrations, that kind of thing."

A British reporter noted about the Humphrey campaign after a July 4 address in Philadelphia: "There is an unmistakable whiff of mediocrity about the Humphrey operation these days." Much of the difficulty lay in Humphrey's organization. The dual leadership of Fred Harris and Walter Mondale had not worked well. Too many Humphrey friends played a part in the campaign without clearly defined responsibilities. He sought to recruit Lawrence O'Brien to play a large role in the organization, but even when O'Brien joined the campaign there still were no clear lines of authority.

The central problem for Humphrey was his relationship to Lyndon Johnson and his position on the war in Vietnam. If the vice president presented himself as a carbon copy of the president, he would inherit all the animosities toward Johnson within the Democratic party and the nation. Yet to split with the president risked a public repudiation and perhaps Johnson's own reentry into the race. Taking a position different from the administration on Vietnam also raised the prospect of attacks on Humphrey for undermining the war effort at a crucial point in the negotiations then under way in Paris.

At some basic level, Humphrey was afraid of Lyndon Johnson. The president had a streak of sadistic cruelty in his personality that he often vented against Humphrey. He told Joseph Califano, a White House aide, that Humphrey had "Minnesota running-water disease. I've never known anyone from Minnesota that could keep their mouth shut." He had promised Humphrey in 1964 that the vice president would have an important role in the administration, but then did all he could to turn Humphrey into a docile and quiet presence. "With Johnson," said a Humphrey worker, "it was either a bear hug or a kick in the ass." Humphrey had decided in 1965 that he was "going to be absolutely loyal to Lyndon Johnson, come what may." Now his future depended on breaking these ties and establishing himself as his own man.

Humphrey held some advantages in a possible confrontation. Johnson could not fire him as vice president, and being the object of the president's wrath would arouse public sympathy. The act of defiance would underline Humphrey's personal courage. But none of these considerations swayed Humphrey. He could not summon the nerve to confront Johnson on the issue. "I'm in the position of walking on a tightrope," he said during the summer of 1968.

Lyndon Johnson did not make Humphrey's political life any easier during these months. Having renounced the presidency and the power he loved, Johnson sought to achieve a Vietnam settlement on his own terms. He did not wish to see the Democratic party and its candidate undercut the White House, and he exercised presidential influence during these months to keep Humphrey in line with the administration. One act of self-denial in 1968 was all that Lyndon Johnson could muster.

One way Johnson damaged his vice president was in the Supreme Court appointments he announced in late June. Chief Justice Earl Warren had informed the president that he intended to resign. To succeed the liberal chief justice, Johnson decided to elevate his old friend Abe Fortas, already an associate justice on the Court. Since promoting Fortas would leave a vacancy, Johnson decided to appoint another close friend, Homer Thornberry of the Fifth Circuit Court of Appeals. The president regarded Fortas as a man of superior intellect, and Johnson thought he could thus influence the direction of the Court well into the future. Since the Senate had already confirmed Fortas for the Supreme Court and Thornberry for a federal judgeship, Johnson reasoned that a majority of senators could hardly balk at this package deal. When Clark Clifford expressed doubts about getting the two men through the Senate, and suggested pairing Fortas with a Republican, Johnson responded, "Well, I don't intend to put some damned Republican on the Court."

Johnson had miscalculated. Both Fortas and Thornberry were politically vulnerable. Fortas had alienated the right wing of the Republican party by representing alleged communists during the 1950s and by some of his decisions on the Court. An equally important weakness was the intimate working relationship he had maintained with Johnson for years, even while Fortas was a sitting justice. He had advised the president on Vietnam policy, drafted speeches, and participated in other policy deliberations. Neither Fortas nor Johnson had been sensitive to the proprieties of his respective position. Charges of cronyism thus had a good deal of substance. In a different sense, the same allegation could be made about Homer Thornberry. He was a decent man whose abilities did not mark him out for a Supreme Court appointment; his rise had been based on his friendship with the president.

In the larger context of 1968, the Fortas nomination offered Republicans a chance to talk about the rulings of the Supreme Court, particularly in the area of criminal law. During the 1960s the Court had expanded the rights of the accused in such cases as *Miranda v. Arizona* (1966), in which the Court held that potential criminal defendants must be informed of their rights before being questioned by the police. Fortas was one of the majority votes in *Miranda*. Before his appointment to the Court, Fortas had defended Clarence Earl Gideon in another case that established the right of every defendant to legal representation.

Nixon did not criticize the Fortas appointment directly. He did not have to. Statements like the one he made to the platform committee of the Republican National Convention sounded the theme in general terms. "At every level of law enforcement and criminal justice," he wrote, "there are needed men with an awareness of the severity of the crime crisis, men with a new attitude toward crime and criminals." Conservative Republicans knew that Nixon would silently support their attack on Fortas.

Johnson lined up Senate votes for his choices, including Republican leader Everett Dirksen. Opposition to Fortas appeared, however, among other Republican senators, most notably Robert P. Griffin of Michigan, who argued that a lame-duck president should not have the right to select two Supreme Court justices. Criticism also focused on Fortas's decisions and on the general issue of "cronyism." Richard Nixon told reporters, "It would have been wise for the President to have delayed the appointment...until the new President had been elected."

In the context of electoral politics, the Fortas nomination aroused partisan feelings among Republicans that a wheeler-dealer president was trying to put something over on their party before the voters could speak. The Senate hearings on Fortas's qualifications allowed Republicans such as Strom Thurmond to work over the issues of liberal "permissiveness" and crime in the streets to the detriment of Democrats. The last thing Hubert Humphrey needed was to have

Lyndon Johnson give the Republicans another reason to be united in their quest for the White House.

Humphrey's clumsy efforts to distance himself from Johnson over Vietnam failed in the weeks before the Democratic National Convention. He indicated to reporters in mid-July that he would soon make an important statement on the war. A group of advisers had been working on a draft pronouncement for a month, and on July 25 they hammered out a final version. In it Humphrey was to say that given positive actions toward deescalation by the enemy, "I would favor an immediate halt in the bombing of North Vietnam."

Humphrey took the draft statement to Johnson that evening, and the president threw cold water on Humphrey's initiative. As Humphrey related, Johnson told him "that I would be jeopardizing the lives of his sons-in-law (then assigned to duty in Vietnam), and endangering the chances of peace. If I announced this, he'd destroy me for the Presidency." A battered Humphrey returned to his aides with the lame excuse that Johnson had been entertaining guests and could not discuss the statement.

Two weeks later, on August 9, Humphrey and Johnson met again at the Johnson ranch in Texas. Richard Nixon had been nominated for president by the Republicans a day earlier. A new draft of a Vietnam statement had been prepared for Humphrey to show the president. It called for an end to the bombing of North Vietnam when the other side showed "reciprocity." Again Johnson was scathing. "You can get a headline with this, Hubert, and it will please you and some of your friends. But if you just let me work for peace, you'll have a better chance for election than by any speech you're going to make. I think I can pull it off. I think that I possibly can get negotiations going, and possibly get the beginnings of peace." With this Hubert Humphrey had to be content as the national convention neared in late August.

While Humphrey struggled with his Vietnam demons, Richard Nixon had moved toward what seemed an inevitable nomination at the Republican National Convention in Miami Beach. At fifty-five years of age, Nixon knew that 1968 would be his last chance at the White House. If he lost another presidential race, there was no possibility the Republicans would turn to him again. Nixon had been a rising young Republican politician during the late 1940s and early 1950s, and that had enabled him to become Eisenhower's running mate in 1952. Early in his career, Nixon was a hard-hitting partisan who waged aggressive, often dirty campaigns against his Democratic opponents. Memories of his use of anticommunism tactics to defeat Helen Gahagan Douglas in the 1950 Senate race in California still roiled older Democrats. During the 1950s Nixon had carried the banners of conservative Republicanism in congressional elections while President Eisenhower remained above the political battles. His narrow defeat at the hands of John Kennedy in 1960 and the loss of the California governorship in 1962 had given him a "loser" image that he struggled hard to overcome during the first half of 1968.

Richard Nixon has been the subject of political and personal analysis for almost half a century. In 1968 that process was especially intense. Had a "New Nixon," the press asked, replaced the "Old Nixon" of the 1950s? The candidate was aware of his problem. "They still call me

'Tricky Dick.' It's a brutal thing to fight...," he said in 1967. The only way he could counter the impression of being devious, Nixon said, was "by absolute candor."

In its handling of the press, the Nixon campaign sought the appearance of candor in the context of tight control. During the primaries Nixon's men found that putting their candidate before favorable audiences that posed friendly questions worked effectively. The resulting footage made for commercials that presented Nixon in a favorable and attractive light. As one aide put it, without irony, they sought to emphasize Nixon's spontaneity, which they could then "capture and capsule."

Because of his lead among Republicans, Nixon could focus on general election issues. The primaries enabled him to test and develop themes for the fall in a way that Hubert Humphrey never could. The relative absence of internal warfare among the Republicans was a significant element in their favor in 1968. It also promised Nixon a united party during the fall campaign, an advantage denied to Humphrey.

After his many years devoted to politics and party, Nixon could count on a network of loyal supporters among Republicans across the country. He was, wrote the novelist Norman Mailer, "the representative" of the "conservative orderly heart" of Midwestern and Far Western Republicanism. Nonetheless, his candidacy aroused more respect than enthusiasm within the GOP in 1968. He was "the one" for the Republicans that year in order to avoid the hated Rockefeller. Many in the South preferred to give their hearts to the more exciting and charismatic Ronald Reagan.

To pursue the presidency, Nixon had assembled a campaign organization designed to avoid the mistakes he had made eight years earlier. "We started Nixon off in 1960 sick and under medication and then we ran his tail off," wrote H. R. Haldeman, one of his senior advisers. It was an error that Nixon and the men around him were determined not to repeat. Their operation also had the luxury of ample resources, with some $10 million available during the preconvention phase of the campaign. Even after a lifetime in politics, the reclusive Nixon did not relish the process of seeking the presidency. When an aide asked if he enjoyed the campaign, the candidate responded, "Never do. Campaigns are something to get over with."

The delegate selection process seemed to favor him strongly. Nelson Rockefeller's expensive attempt to show Nixon's weaknesses in the polls had produced no significant results. Meanwhile, delegates moved toward Nixon. He won the Illinois primary and did well in the New Mexico, Washington, and Montana state conventions. Capping off the favorable trend, former president Dwight D. Eisenhower endorsed him on July 18. From his sickbed in Washington, Eisenhower told the press of his "admiration of [Nixon's] personal qualities."

With the nomination seemingly in hand, Nixon had time to work on his acceptance speech and to think about his running mate. Nixon wanted his vice-presidential candidate to be more effective than Henry Cabot Lodge had been in 1960. On several occasions Lodge had embarrassed Nixon and hurt the campaign against Kennedy. One name that came up frequently in Nixon's inner circle was that of Spiro T. Agnew, the governor of Maryland. The idea was tucked away for future consideration.

As the summer progressed, Nixon pursued his campaign on several different levels. In addition to winning delegates, he looked ahead to the general election. What Nixon most feared politically was that Lyndon Johnson might achieve the appearance of peace in Vietnam on the eve of the election. Accordingly, Nixon moved carefully to identify himself with the goals of the president's policy on Vietnam, "even though I would be critical of some of the tactics that had been used." Nixon received an intelligence briefing at the White House on July 26, a courtesy that Johnson provided to all the presidential hopefuls. He told the president he would not "undercut our negotiating position just in case the Communists came around and agreed to the conditions Johnson would insist upon in return for a bombing halt." A day earlier Johnson had quashed Humphrey's effort to separate himself from the administration on Vietnam. Now here was Nixon apparently supporting the White House. Two days before Nixon's visit, Johnson told Clark Clifford and Dean Rusk, "The GOP may be of more help to us than the Democrats in the next few months." What Nixon said strengthened Johnson's view that he was closer to the president's position than was Humphrey.

Unbeknown to the president, Nixon and his campaign had already made a contact with Vietnam that would prove crucial during the waning days of the election. Anna Chennault was the widow of General Claire Chennault, who had led the famous Flying Tigers squadron in China during World War II. Of Chinese ancestry, Mrs. Chennault had become identified with the Republican party during the 1960s, and she counted many friends among South Vietnamese political leaders in Saigon and Washington. In late June she wrote to candidate Nixon saying that the ambassador to the United States from South Vietnam, Bui Diem, was "my close friend." She urged Nixon to meet with him.

Nixon told aides that "if it can be [secret]" he would like to see Diem. If secrecy could not be maintained, an aide should handle the meeting. According to Mrs. Chennault's memoir, Nixon had already met the ambassador some months earlier. In any event, the channel was well established by mid-summer 1968, to be used in case Nixon needed to convey a private message to the South Vietnamese government. As Nixon told Bui Diem, "If you have any message for me, please give it to Anna and she will relay it to me and I will do the same in the future."

For the moment, however, Nixon's thoughts were on the Republican convention to be held August 5 to 9. While his managers assured him, as John Mitchell said, that "we've got everything under control," he knew that Nelson Rockefeller and Ronald Reagan were maneuvering to show delegates that Nixon could be stopped, that a first-ballot victory was not a foregone conclusion. As the convention neared, Nixon knew that Rockefeller's challenge would fail. Despite the money the New York governor had thrown into his polling campaign, in Nixon's words, "his efforts seemed to have minimal effect." The potential of a Reagan candidacy was more worrisome. Throughout the primary campaign, Reagan had always been perceived as the main alternative to a Nixon nomination.

Ronald Reagan had burst upon the national political scene in 1966 when he defeated the incumbent Democratic governor of California, Edmund G. "Pat" Brown, by almost a million votes. His ability to thrill the hearts of conservative Republicans had been evident two years earlier when his televised speech in favor of Barry Goldwater had been the hit of the faltering Republican presidential campaign. A former Democrat who had become famous as an actor in movies and television, Reagan was a gifted speaker with the ability to state the conservative creed in crisp and forceful phrases. "There are simple answers," he told Californians in 1966, "just not easy ones." He promised a smaller state government, lower taxes, and a crackdown on those who abused welfare and other government programs. His smashing victory over Brown gave Reagan instant visibility as a potential Republican presidential aspirant.

Reagan came to the California governorship with no experience in government, and in his first two years he suffered some rocky moments. In 1967 he was forced to seek a significant tax increase from the legislature to pay for the increasing costs of state services that had resisted his economy measures that seemed so attractive in the campaign. In that same year a scandal uncovered homosexuals on the governor's staff. Nonetheless, Reagan demonstrated impressive abilities as a fund-raiser among Republicans; he could bring in several hundred thousand dollars during a swing through several states. His rhetoric stirred the blood of the party faithful. "We can't really blame the President alone for the mess we're in," he jibed. "A mess like that takes teamwork."

Reagan had no desire to take on Nixon directly in 1968. He had said during his campaign that he would not use the governorship as a stepping-stone to the presidency. He controlled the large California delegation to the national convention, and as a "favorite son" he would be put in nomination whether he campaigned openly or not. Yet if he was perceived as a declared candidate, he would be measured in the polls against Nixon, where he was bound to fare badly. His best approach was to accept the many speaking invitations that came his way, raise money for the party, and allow his friends quietly to court potential delegates on his behalf. If Nixon ran into trouble, or if a deadlocked convention loomed, Reagan's candidacy would prosper.

The Reagan campaign moved carefully during the early months of 1968. His name appeared on the ballot in those states where officials moved to place it, and he declined to insist that his name be removed. Reagan gained 11 percent of the vote in Wisconsin's primary in April, rose to 22 percent in the Nebraska primary, and prepared to do even better in the Oregon balloting in late May. Reagan supporters spent some $200,000 on television advertising in Oregon, including a documentary, "Ronald Reagan: Citizen Governor." But the Reagan drive stalled when the governor received only 23 percent of the vote to Nixon's 73 percent. Despite this setback, Reagan continued to be a threat to Nixon's chances. "There was always a possibility," Nixon wrote later, "that Southern delegates could be lured at the last minute by his ideological siren song."

During the week before the start of the Republican convention, the platform committee debated how the party should approach the issues before the voters. Under the leadership of Senator Dirksen, the GOP offered stern criticism of Lyndon Johnson's domestic policies while adopting a cautious line on the Vietnam War. "Lawlessness is crumbling the foundations of American society," the platform asserted, and it pledged "vigorous and evenhanded administration of justice and enforcement of the law." As for Vietnam, it offered "a program for peace" that would be "neither peace at any price nor a camouflaged surrender of legitimate United States or allied interests." Instead the Republicans promised "a fair and equitable settlement to all, based on the principle of self-determination, our national interests and the cause of long-range world peace." They also said their course would "enable and induce South Vietnam to assume increasing responsibility." The goal was "a progressive de-Americanization of the war, both military and civilian." Rather than calling for further U.S. prosecution of the war, the Republican platform advocated what Richard Nixon would later describe as "Vietnamization" of the conflict.

As the convention prepared to open on August 5, Ronald Reagan made his unofficial candidacy official. In a staged event with the California delegation, his supporters adopted a resolution that asked the governor to become "a leading and bona fide candidate for President." Reagan walked in and commented, "Gosh, I was surprised. It all came out of the clear blue sky." Now the issue turned on whether Reagan could break into Nixon's support among Southern Republicans. Reagan's campaign manager, F. Clifton White, told reporters, "All we need is just one break—one state switching to Reagan—and we've got him."

The strategy for Nixon's two main opponents was to prevent his victory on the first ballot. If they could do that, the strength of the front-runner would wane and compromise candidates could emerge. Nelson Rockefeller believed he would then win in the end. A more likely scenario, given the anti-Rockefeller passions that ran through the convention, would have been a Reagan victory. For the moment, however, there was an uneasy and unspoken alliance against Nixon between the moderate Rockefeller and the conservative Reagan.

The issue on which the well-organized Nixon operation could falter was the vice presidency. If he decided to select a Northern liberal, such as John Lindsay of New York or Mark Hatfield of Oregon, unhappy Southerners might defect and switch their votes to Reagan. Newspaper stories circulated that Lindsay and Hatfield were under active consideration. Such trial balloons from the Nixon camp triggered fear among the conservative Southern delegates, and by the evening of Monday, August 5, the Nixon camp was hearing reports of possible gains for Reagan in Dixie. When the leader of the North Carolina delegation told Nixon operatives, "I'm for Ronnie," concern rose among members of the Nixon high command. Southern supporters warned of a need "to see Nixon tonight" because "things are taking a turn for the worse."

That evening Nixon met with Strom Thurmond and Harry Dent of South Carolina and repeated his pledges that the vice-presidential nominee would be someone acceptable to the South. He also reaffirmed that he opposed "civil wrongs" and would appoint an attorney general "who'll enforce the law!" On the emotional issue of how to desegregate schools in the South, Nixon made clear his firm opposition to busing. His visitors told Nixon to repeat those same positions to Southern delegates when he met with them the next morning.

How Nixon handled the racial questions would be central to the success of his campaign. To appeal to the South, especially the border states, he had to be more conciliatory to whites than Hubert Humphrey would be. At the same time he could not outbid George Wallace for racist voters North and South, or he would face an uproar among Northern Republicans and moderate Democrats. What Nixon did was to reaffirm his support for the principles of integration in general but remain cautious about the use of federal power to push racial change. His emphasis rested on voluntary compliance by the South with an even-handed racial policy.

To avoid being trapped at either extreme of the racial

question, Nixon had spoken in favor of the open-housing legislation proposed by the White House after the death of Martin Luther King. Nixon was not an admirer of the open-housing law, but he thought, as he later informed Southern delegates, that it was best "to get the civil-rights and open-housing issues out of our sight so we didn't have a split party over the platform when we came down here to Miami Beach."

On the issues of school desegregation and busing, circumstances played into Nixon's hands during the spring of 1968. The Supreme Court ruled in May that the "freedom-of-choice" approach to school integration had failed to end dual school systems in the South. It was not enough for parents to have the right to choose where their children would go to school. To end segregation it would be necessary, the decision seemed to say, to transport children to other schools in their districts in order to achieve proper racial balance.

In light of the Court's ruling, Southern Republicans were exercised about the prospect of the federal government setting "guidelines" for the pursuit of integration. Nixon worked out a strategy designed to say just what his white supporters in the South wanted to hear without descending to the levels where George Wallace operated so well. At meetings with the Southern delegates, he ran through his positions with the skill he had so often displayed in such group settings. One of the delegates carried a small tape recorder, and the candidate's remarks were preserved and published the next day in the *Miami Herald*.

Nixon said first that he would not select anyone as his running mate who "is going to divide the party." On busing, he assured delegates that he opposed moving "the child—a child that is two or three grades behind another child—into a strange community." He attacked federal judges who overruled the decisions of local school districts or school boards. "I think it is the job of the courts to interpret the law, and not make the law." On Vietnam he promised "a massive training program so that the South Vietnamese can be trained to take over the fighting—that they can be phased in as we phase out."

The sessions with the Southern delegates went even better than the Nixon camp might have anticipated. By the time Nixon finished, Reagan's hoped-for gains in Southern support had been largely canceled. It was clear that Thurmond and other Nixon supporters would be able to deliver the Southern Republicans for him on the first ballot. Reagan tried to sway Thurmond without success on Tuesday. As the delegates prepared to ballot on Wednesday, August 7, it looked as though Nixon had withstood the Reagan challenge.

But there were still pitfalls. When the Florida delegation began to waver, Strom Thurmond had to make a personal visit to ask them to hold off their sentiment for Ronald Reagan. Similar signs of Reagan sentiment appeared within the Alabama delegation, but that rebellion ended after the Nixon forces offered minor concessions. To compensate for any losses in the South, the Nixon campaign made inroads into the New Jersey delegation to draw off potential Rockefeller support. Even as the nominating speeches began, another round of Reagan sentiment surfaced when the *Miami Herald* reported that Nixon would select Mark Hatfield as his running mate. Nixon leaders in the South confronted the reporter who had written the story and challenged him to bet several hundred dollars on its accuracy. When the reporter refused, the news spread quickly among Nixon supporters in Dixie.

Republicans spent ten hours nominating their candidates. Spiro T. Agnew of Maryland nominated Nixon as a man "firm in upholding the law and determined in the pursuit of justice." Nixon "knows what is needed to be President and he knows what a President needs to be." Reagan and Rockefeller were also placed in nomination, along with a bevy of favorite-son candidates such as George Romney, Winthrop Rockefeller, and Hiram Fong. When the balloting began, the states fell into place as the Nixon people had forecast. The final totals gave Nixon 692 votes to 277 for Rockefeller and 182 for Reagan. Nixon had won the nomination with 25 votes to spare.

Nixon watched the returns on television in his hotel suite, tabulating the vote on one of the yellow pads he used for drafting memos and speeches. "We had come halfway up the mountain," he said later. Congratulatory phone calls soon started flowing in, including one from Nelson Rockefeller who told him that Reagan "didn't come through as well as we expected."

The first task for the Republican nominee was the selection of his vice-presidential candidate. Although Nixon had decided several weeks before the convention that Spiro T. Agnew was the likely choice, "like most important decisions, this one would not be final until it was announced." Nixon very much wanted to avoid duplicating the mistake he had made in 1960 when he ran with Henry Cabot Lodge, Jr., of Massachusetts. In 1968 the vice-presidential choice should be someone who would help the ticket, attract votes in the South and border states, and follow the lead of the Nixon campaign.

Spiro Agnew seemed to have these qualities in 1968. He was fifty years old, the son of Greek immigrant parents, and a veteran of World War II who had practiced

law in Maryland during the 1950s. In 1960 he decided
to enter Republican politics and ran unsuccessfully for
a judgeship. He was elected a county executive in Baltimore in 1962 and ran for governor four years later. In the
election campaign Agnew's opponent, George P. Mahoney,
was a Democrat who opposed the integration of housing in
the state. His slogan was, "Your Home Is Your Castle."
Mahoney's segregationist posture split the Democrats and
opened the way for the election of the more moderate
Agnew.

In 1968 Agnew seemed a likely supporter of Nelson
Rockefeller. He was one of the few Republican governors
who was prepared to come out publicly for the New
Yorker during the spring. Then Rockefeller suddenly decided on March 21 not to make the race. Before he
made the announcement, he did not call Agnew and prepare him for what was about to happen. As a result,
Agnew was embarrassed. He had invited reporters to his
office to see the anticipated Rockefeller entrance into
the race. Instead he was humiliated. "It made him look
like a horse's ass," said one Republican. Agnew began to
move toward Nixon. He also changed his mind about some
of the racial issues that had brought him to the governor's
office.

After the death of Martin Luther King, Maryland had its
share of rioting in the wake of the assassination. Agnew
mobilized the National Guard and requested federal troops
to maintain order in the state. At a meeting with black
leaders in his office, Agnew scolded them for their behavior
and accused them of being parties to the rioting. Most of the
blacks in attendance walked out of the session. Agnew
followed up with statements that showed his new feelings.
"Policemen ought to shoot looters who fail to halt when

ordered," he said. He also charged that urban rioting grew out of "the misguided compassion of public opinion." A governor who had won election against a segregationist rival was now saying that crime and permissiveness should be dealt with harshly. It was a combination that "fit perfectly with the strategy we had devised for the November election," Nixon recalled.

Nixon had weighed Agnew's political strengths and weaknesses with a masterful sense of electoral reality. Despite the importance of the vice presidency as a national office, however, Nixon ordered no probe of Agnew's private affairs or his finances. Nor did Nixon ask him whether he had any potential embarrassments that might affect his fitness to be vice president. It was a significant oversight. During Nixon's presidency, federal investigators discovered evidence that Agnew was involved in conspiracies to commit bribery, extortion, and tax fraud. During his service in Maryland government Agnew had regularly received payments and kickbacks from contractors in his state. These payments continued while Agnew was a vice-presidential candidate and even during his service under Nixon. Eventually they would lead to Agnew's resignation as vice president in 1973.

In August 1968, however, the issue was how Agnew would help the Nixon candidacy. Nixon offered the vice-presidential slot first to his old friend from California, Robert Finch, but Finch declined. Nixon then asked Congressman Rogers Morton from Maryland. Morton also said no, arguing that "Ted [Agnew] would be the stronger candidate." Nixon then rapidly settled on Agnew, announcing it to a press corps on August 8 that reacted with "absolute shock and surprise." There was a brief flurry of opposition to Agnew in the convention, but it rapidly disappeared. His opponents mustered only 178 delegates against his nomination.

Agnew's selection proved to be a source of political trouble for Nixon during the campaign. Agnew had a tendency to speak without thinking, and his off-the-cuff remarks produced several episodes that Democrats exploited. It is not clear that Agnew added much strength to the ticket, though he may have been helpful in the border states.

For Nixon the climax of the national convention was to be his speech accepting the nomination. No campaign speech would "have a larger or more attentive audience." Events outside the convention hall reinforced the arguments Nixon would make. The night before, while Nixon's nomination was being won, blacks in nearby Miami's Liberty City ghetto had rioted. Three black residents died, and troops were called into the area to put down looting and sniping. The episode symbolized the tensions within the nation in 1968. In the opulent confines of Miami Beach, well protected from any disturbances, the delegates went about choosing the next president; ten miles away, the social problems of the nation burst open once again.

Nixon's acceptance speech was a mixture of his familiar campaign address and some personal comments about his own life. The product of many speech writers, it reflected Nixon's perceptions about what the voters wanted to hear from a Republican candidate. He spoke for "the great majority of Americans, the forgotten Americans, the non-shouters, the nondemonstrators." He then made the case for "new leadership." The nation was "tied down for four years in a war in Vietnam with no end in sight." The United States could not "manage its own economy" and was "plagued by unprecedented racial violence." He jabbed at

Johnson and the Great Society without mentioning the president's name. "I say it's time to quit pouring billions of dollars into programs that have failed." He promised to appoint a new attorney general who would be tough on crime.

In closing he invoked the plight of children who failed to benefit from the American dream. When those children awoke each morning, he said, they encountered "a living nightmare of poverty, neglect, and despair." Having sketched that difficult social problem, he then turned to the story of another child who "hears a train go by. At night he dreams of faraway places where he'd like to go. It seems like an impossible dream." But with the help of family and friends, Richard Nixon prevailed in "his chosen profession of politics," and "tonight he stands before you, nominated for President of the United States of America."

The Republican convention had done everything Nixon wanted it to accomplish. The party was united behind his candidacy, and there had been no major divisive battle to weaken the national campaign. Nixon received what pollsters call a "bounce" from the convention: he held a strong lead of 45 percent to 29 percent over Hubert Humphrey in the Gallup poll. George Wallace trailed with 18 percent of the vote. The choice of Agnew had aroused some controversy, but Nixon expected that his running mate would play well in the border states against Wallace.

By 1968 the Republican party was on the verge of dominating the competition for electoral votes. In much of the West the Republicans had little to fear from the Democrats. Nixon could reasonably expect to start out with as many as 65 to 70 electoral votes in the Far West and Great Plains states. He was also virtually assured of the votes of such Midwestern states as Iowa, Indiana, and Ohio. He hoped to run well in the industrial states of New York, Illinois, Pennsylvania, and Michigan, and he was intent on carrying California and Texas. The key to Nixon's chances lay in the South. If he could blunt the challenge of George Wallace, he would gain the 268 electoral votes he needed for election.

Turning back the Wallace candidacy would not be easy. Southern Republicans warned Nixon that Wallace was doing well with voters who would otherwise support the GOP. Nixon knew he could not outbid Wallace on the race issue; his task was to persuade voters that casting their ballots for Wallace was futile. "Our message to would-be Wallace voters," Nixon remembered, "was 'Don't Waste Your Vote.' "

The Nixon campaign was well financed. The Republican party contributed something over $7 million, and the Nixon-Agnew campaign itself raised another $23 million. Nixon's finance director, Maurice Stans, later observed that "ours was the most expensive campaign ever." During the 1960s the base of small contributors developed by Ray Bliss gave Republicans a decided edge over Democrats. In 1968 big contributors also poured in money to see that Republicans regained the White House. Clement Stone of Chicago, a friend of Nixon's, gave more than $200,000 while hotel magnate J. Willard Marriott added $103,000. Republicans had all the money they needed to wage a modern campaign in contrast to underfunded Democrats. Nixon told his staff, "Be sure we outspend them on television, especially in the last three weeks. Remember '60—I never want to be outspent again."

Nixon and his men had ample reason to be confident as they surveyed the campaign after their party's convention.

They had a well-tested organization, an effective candidate, and a disorganized opposition. Their advantages actually grew during the remainder of August as the Democrats moved toward a disastrous national convention of their own. Yet there was an underlying weakness at the heart of the Nixon campaign that would prove significant as the election neared. As William Safire, a Nixon speech writer, observed, "Nixon was playing not to lose." His candidacy rested on the premise that the voters wanted a change from the Democrats and would inevitably turn to Nixon. Thus there was the ambiguous campaign slogan, "Nixon's the One." The emptiness of the appeal was evident in the song that went everywhere with the candidate: "Nixon's the One / Nixon's the One / Nixon's the One for Me."

As long as the Nixon campaign was comfortably ahead in the polls and confident of success, the lack of a clear, positive message was irrelevant. But if Democrats found unity and purpose, and began to close the gap on Republicans, the absence of a central theme might prove to be more of a problem than the Nixon men had anticipated. Such a problem seemed far away during the confident days of August 1968. "It is essential that we maintain the initiative," Nixon instructed his associates on September 5. "We must play the confident line from now until November, regardless of what developments occur."

As Republicans readied themselves for the fall campaign, Democrats prepared for their convention. Originally scheduled as a celebration of Lyndon Johnson's sixtieth birthday on August 27, the gathering was to be held in Chicago, where the city's colorful and domineering mayor, Richard J. Daley, could provide a friendly setting for what the president had assumed would be a consensus renomination. Those considerations had preceded the striking events of

1968. Now the Democrats were meeting as a divided party with the prospect of bitter floor disputes and even more violent protests outside the convention hall. Yet even the most pessimistic Democrats could not have anticipated the trauma that awaited their party in Chicago.

5

Democratic Disaster at Chicago

By MID-AUGUST Hubert Humphrey was on the verge of winning the Democratic presidential nomination. The vice president was well ahead of Eugene McCarthy in the polls and in the race for convention delegates. Journalists estimated that Humphrey had about 1,250 committed delegates and was within 70 votes of the 1,312 delegates he needed. McCarthy had at most 800 delegates and little chance of winning on his own. The death of Robert Kennedy had left the Democrats' antiwar wing divided and frustrated.

Despite these favorable signs, Humphrey's position was vulnerable and uncertain. Following the Republican convention he trailed Richard Nixon by sixteen percentage points in the polls. His own campaign was disorganized and underfunded, and he had not been able to heal the splits in his party. Audiences at Humphrey's speeches were often hostile and jeering. Most of all, the vice president still had not resolved his relationship to Lyndon Johnson and the president's war policies. Humphrey had almost no influence on the negotiations the White House was conducting with North Vietnam and the Soviet Union. He believed that if he broke with Johnson the president could easily destroy his candidacy.

At the same time Johnson had his doubts about Humphrey's loyalty to his administration and his policies. In July the president had told his advisers that Nixon "may prove to be more responsible than the Democrats." When he saw a newspaper photograph of Humphrey and Eugene McCarthy each with a crying baby in his arms, Johnson remarked, "That's the way I feel when I look at the two candidates, like crying." Johnson's meeting with Nixon and Spiro Agnew on August 10 was friendly. The Republican candidate said he would not criticize him on the war if the president did not "soften" his position. Humphrey thus knew the dangers of challenging Johnson directly. Yet the closer he remained to the president, the worse his electoral position became.

Humphrey's other problem was the national convention in Chicago on August 26. The site and date for the convention had been set months earlier when Lyndon Johnson was still a likely candidate for reelection. Mayor Richard Daley of Chicago had lobbied hard with the president during the fall of 1967 to have his city selected. The president could carry Illinois if the party met in Chicago, Daley contended. Although the television networks wanted both parties to meet in Miami to save money, and although security would be easier in the Florida city, Johnson went with Daley and decided to hold the convention in late August. Thus the delegates could celebrate Lyndon Johnson's sixtieth birthday on August 27.

In hindsight the choice of Chicago was a political disaster. The timing produced severe difficulties for Humphrey and the Democrats. The Republicans, meeting several weeks earlier, had plenty of time to launch their campaign smoothly and efficiently in early September. By the time Humphrey was nominated, he had only a weekend to ready himself for the traditional start of the campaign on Labor Day. Since the vice president and his staff had done virtually no planning for the general election before the convention, the Democrats went into the decisive phase of the 1968 election with no clear sense of strategy for the campaign. An earlier convention would have given them time to raise money and to settle their plans.

In the weeks before the convention Democratic disunity intensified. Senator George S. McGovern of South Dakota entered the presidential race on August 10. Because of his closeness to the Kennedys, his candidacy seemed designed to hold the former supporters of Robert Kennedy together until the convention. There was now the hope among these delegates that Senator Edward M. Kennedy might accept a draft. McGovern's announcement underlined the perception that neither Humphrey nor McCarthy had strong appeal to the Kennedy faction of the party.

By August many liberal Democrats believed the election could not be won unless their party moved away from the administration's position on Vietnam. Yet the president gave them little reason to expect a change in his views. He had conferred with President Nguyen Van Thieu of South Vietnam in mid-July in Hawaii. At a press conference Johnson characterized the "big rumors" that the meeting was "to discuss stopping the bombing or to pull out" as "just pure, absolute tommyrot and fiction." In other public statements he repeated his unwillingness to "order the cessation of unilateral acts of bombing of the infiltration routes" being used by the North Vietnamese. On August 19, a week before the national convention, he told the Veterans of Foreign Wars in Detroit, "We are not going to stop the bombing just to give them [North Vietnam] a chance to step up their bloodbath."

Johnson's adamant stance did not deter prominent Democrats from searching for some way to have the party's platform distance the nominee from the unpopular war. The McCarthy camp took the most radical position on the issue. Their proposed plank on Vietnam, announced on August 17, came out for an "unconditional end to all the bombing of North Vietnam," a negotiated withdrawal of all United States and North Vietnamese troops from South Vietnam, a coalition government in South Vietnam, and reduced military action on the battlefield. Johnson's Detroit speech indicated that the administration would never accept what McCarthy and his allies were proposing. The White House had firm control of the platform committee through its chair, Congressman Hale Boggs of Louisiana.

An effort continued, however, to find language that the antiwar faction could support, that Humphrey could run on, and that the White House would accept. These discussions opened on August 1 at a Washington hotel. A consensus emerged among the Kennedy men, McCarthy supporters, and the McGovern delegates present that they had to be flexible and creative in working out platform language. By the time the platform committee convened on August 19, the advocates of a peace plank had worked out wording that Humphrey might find useful. The proposal included a call for an end to the bombing and a negotiated withdrawal from the war.

Outside events soon weakened the peace initiative. On August 20 Soviet troops invaded Czechoslovakia to extinguish its reformist government that had emerged during the "Prague spring." This aggressive move undercut Johnson's plans for an East-West summit. The president had hoped to announce agreements with Moscow as a way of stressing the peace issue in the campaign and ending his administration on an upbeat note. Worse still for the peace forces, the invasion strengthened the hands of those who contended that any negotiations with communist governments were inherently dangerous. Senator McCarthy added to the political damage when he described the invasion as "not a major crisis." His assessment was accurate in a diplomatic sense—the United States could do nothing but protest the Soviet action; but the senator's words suggested that antiwar Democrats lacked a full appreciation of the dangers that confronted the United States during the summer of 1968.

In any event, Lyndon Johnson would not tolerate a platform critical of his Vietnam policy. He had his own plans for bringing about negotiations and an end to the bombing of North Vietnam, and he wanted no interference from liberal Democrats. Through his operatives on the scene in Chicago, including Postmaster General Marvin Watson, he made sure the administration position was endorsed. On August 26, the day the convention opened, the president insisted that the language of the platform specify that any bombing halt would occur only "*when* this action would not endanger the lives of our troops in the field; this action should take into account the response from Hanoi." Critics of the president believed this formulation offered the North Vietnamese slight incentive to accept.

In a conversation with Johnson that same day, Humphrey argued that the plank worked out between his aides and the liberals was "acceptable and not offensive." Johnson's response was simple and definitive: "This plank undercuts our whole policy and, by God, the Democratic party ought not to be doing that to me, and you ought not to be doing it; you've been a part of this policy." Given how little influence Humphrey had exercised on Vietnam policy as vice president, this last assertion must have been ironic for him.

Humphrey briefly thought about making a determined stand on the platform issue. He retreated when Hale Boggs threatened to resign as chair of the platform committee if confronted with a plank that the president deemed unacceptable. In hindsight, Humphrey wrote, "I should not have yielded." Worked on by Richard Nixon's shrewd courting of him on Vietnam, and defensive about his own place in history, the president showed little party loyalty by August 1968. He even toyed briefly with an improbable renomination if Humphrey faltered further. Wisely, Lyndon Johnson decided he could not go to the convention. His presence would have made an ugly situation even more explosive.

As it unfolded, the Democratic convention visited disaster after disaster upon the party. Efforts to find an alternative to Humphrey led to an abortive attempt to draft Senator Edward M. Kennedy of Massachusetts as the natural heir of the legacy of his two dead brothers. Grief-stricken by the year's events and aware of his own lack of qualifications for the presidency, the thirty-six-year-old Kennedy wondered what to do about the sentiment for a draft that welled up in the weeks before the convention. In the end it came down to whether Eugene McCarthy would withdraw in favor of Kennedy. McCarthy said he would like to see his name placed in nomination, then he would withdraw in favor of Kennedy. "While I am doing this for Teddy," he said to Kennedy's brother-in-law Stephen Smith, "I never could have done it for Bobby." The remark probably convinced Smith and Kennedy that they could not trust McCarthy to go through with such an understanding. On Wednesday, August 28, the third day of the convention, Kennedy phoned Humphrey to say he would not be a candidate.

Edward Kennedy would never again be as close to the Democratic nomination as he was in August 1968, but it is doubtful that the draft would have been as easy as its adherents thought. Southern Democrats would not have accepted Kennedy under any circumstances, and Humphrey probably would have held on to enough votes to deny the Massachusetts senator the nomination. When the Kennedy boom ended, the chances of finding a liberal alternative to Humphrey also disappeared.

The Democratic convention produced a series of political embarrassments for the party that weakened it for a generation. As a result of the way in which Humphrey's delegates had been chosen in caucuses and state conventions, liberals believed that the party rules had become only a means of frustrating the will of Democrats nationally. They came to Chicago resolved to change the rules of the game, even if they did not succeed in 1968. A group of McCarthy supporters had established a commission to look into the methods of selecting delegates. In many areas there were apparent abuses. Delegates could be chosen up to two years before the convention, and the exact nature of the nominating process was vague in several states.

Particular attention focused on the so-called "unit rule" which allowed majorities in Southern states to control an entire delegation and shut out the party minority altogether. Blacks and liberals saw the unit rule as the last resort of such Southern conservatives as John Connally. The Humphrey camp first told Connally that the unit rule would remain in effect at the 1968 convention and be changed in the future. Then Connally learned that Humphrey, feeling pressure from Northern liberals, had endorsed the abolition of the rule "at this convention." An irate Connally began talking about a possible draft-Johnson movement. To avoid a divisive floor fight, the convention rules committee enacted a "freedom of conscience" provision which allowed delegates covered by the unit rule to vote as they thought best.

Other rules committee action had even more far-reaching effects on Democrats. Meeting on Tuesday, August 27, the committee set up a subcommittee to investigate how delegates were selected and to improve the process. A second subcommittee was empowered to look into enhancing the participation of all Democrats whatever their religion, race, gender, or national origin. The convention approved these initiatives later that same day. During the four years after 1968, the work of these committees would transform the ways in which Democrats chose their presidential nominee. The goal was to make the party more open and more representative; the unintended consequence was to render Democrats less able to pick candidates who could win the White House.

The Democratic convention of 1968 is as famous for what occurred in the streets of Chicago during late August as for the events inside the hall that ended in the nomination of Hubert Humphrey. As police and antiwar protesters confronted each other, passions over the war in Vietnam reshaped national politics with explosive impact. Television cameras carried the anger of the demonstrators and the response of the Chicago police into living rooms across the country. In a year of social unrest, the violence in Chicago symbolized the tensions that threatened to shatter the social order.

As soon as the Democrats announced in late 1967 that their national convention would be held in Chicago, antiwar groups debated whether to stage protest demonstrations in the streets. A lack of money and people meant that only one of the major party conventions could be targeted, and the Democrats seemed the more compelling choice. Johnson was likely to be renominated; in the eyes of those who denounced the war he was the main villain. As one of the more flamboyant protest leaders put it, "Chicago is LBJ's stage and we are going to steal it."

By early 1968 the peace movement against the Vietnam War had undergone significant changes since its emergence on the national scene in mid-1965. Two years of rallies, marches, and several violent protests had produced no discernible shift in the war policies of the Johnson administration. Behind the scenes, as the events of March 1968 showed, there was a good deal of anxiety within the White House about the course of the war. But the protesters saw only that the war they hated went on in Southeast Asia.

A climax to the mass-protest phase of the antiwar campaign came in October 1967 with the March on the Pentagon, organized by the National Mobilization to End the War. About 100,000 people came to Washington. A morning of speeches and entertainment at the Lincoln Memorial led to an afternoon walk to the Pentagon where a confrontation occurred with police and soldiers. Almost 650 marchers were arrested and a number of protesters were beaten. Angry that their tactics had not produced any change in the war policy, leaders of the peace movement told one another that "one of our continuing aims must be to disrupt and block the war machine.... We might discuss the implications of trying to disrupt the nominating conventions of the Republican and Democratic parties."

The groups who planned to assemble in Chicago were diverse and often at cross-purposes with one another. The Youth International Party, or "Yippies," attracted much media attention. The two leading figures of this small fringe organization were Jerry Rubin and Abbie Hoffman. They had been participants in the civil rights and antiwar campaigns but had gradually become convinced that the movement needed new techniques and tactics to gain public attention and approval. Their goal, they said, was the "Politics of Ecstasy."

Abbie Hoffman was thirty-two in 1968, "a small wiry figure with a grotesque balloon of hair." After a degree from Brandeis University in 1959, he attended graduate school briefly and then worked for several years in a state mental hospital in Massachusetts. He spent time in civil rights and antiwar activities but was increasingly drawn to the world of drugs, rock, and what the 1960s called the "counterculture." He lost faith in conventional political organizing and turned instead to street theatre, public relations stunts, and media manipulation. His goals were "Revolution for the hell of it!" and "Theatre in the streets!"

At thirty, Jerry Rubin had shown himself to be an adept creator of the kinds of symbolic protests that Hoffman envisioned. A few inches shorter than his friend, Rubin graduated from the University of Cincinnati, went to graduate school at Berkeley for a few weeks, and then turned to protest politics full time. In 1966 he said, "We are a dangerous country, a neurotic country possessing deadly power." To get beyond the limits of electoral politics and change the attitudes of mainstream America required the devices of mass culture and mass entertainment. "Politics was just a circus," Rubin said, and protest should be entertaining and diverting. The manifesto that announced the birth of the Yippies in January 1968 struck that note. "Join us in Chicago in August for an international festival of youth music and theatre," it proclaimed. "Rise up and abandon the creeping meatball."

During the first half of 1968 Rubin, Hoffman, and their associates gave the national press a diet of sensational threats and stunts that became the trademark of the Yippies. Jerry Rubin forecast that a pig would be nominated for president and then eaten, that the Democratic convention itself could be infiltrated and disrupted, or that mind-altering drugs could be placed in the Chicago water supply. The Yippies proposed "merely an attack of mental disobedience on an obediently insane society." Their fortunes and those of their leaders fluctuated with the tide of political events. When McCarthy and Robert Kennedy were attracting votes in the spring, the appeal of fringe protests faded. As the nomination of Humphrey seemed likely, the Yippies resolved to mount a protest in Chicago. At no time did they command any sort of mass following. But they succeeded in gaining a great deal of press coverage and alerting city and federal authorities to the prospect of erratic protest behavior.

The more conventional and political elements of the antiwar forces approached the Chicago convention at a low point in their fortunes. Johnson's withdrawal from the race, the start of negotiations with the North Vietnamese in Paris, the relative deescalation of the fighting, and the candidacies of McCarthy and Kennedy—all these had drained some of the energies from the antiwar camp.

None of the major party candidates favored an intensification of the fighting. These developments produced disarray among the radical left. During the winter of 1968 they argued at length about whether to stage demonstrations in Chicago at all. Passions were also intense over the question of whether demonstrations should continue to be nonviolent. Should the antiwar forces look to violent action as a way of separating themselves from the liberal Democrats?

Johnson's withdrawal stalled decisions on a strategy for convention demonstrations. It also became clear that Mayor Richard Daley and his police force would not deal gently with protesters. Following the murder of Martin Luther King, Jr., Daley had issued his "shoot-to-kill" order about arsonists, and on April 27 Chicago police had broken up an antiwar rally with clubs and chemical sprays. The marchers, Daley said, were "hoodlums and communists."

After Robert Kennedy's death and McCarthy's faltering presidential campaign, the idea of a demonstration in Chicago revived. By summer Tom Hayden, Rennie Davis, and David Dellinger were the most visible leaders in the planning for protests against the Democrats. Hayden was born in 1939 and educated at the University of Michigan. He had helped to organize Students for a Democratic Society (SDS) and was the principal author of the "Port Huron Statement" which offered a critique of American society in 1962 and a vision of what came to be called "participatory democracy." During the civil rights battles of the early 1960s and the antiwar protests that followed, Hayden emerged as an articulate, celebrated radical personality. He went to North Vietnam in 1965. He came back convinced that the only goal for politics in 1968 was "to make it impossible for the next president to be elected without first agreeing to end the war."

Dellinger was an older member of the peace movement who had opposed American participation in World War II. His belief that "all war is evil and useless" made him a conscientious objector and cost him three years in prison. Dellinger had marched for civil rights and then turned naturally to opposition to Vietnam. In 1967, at fifty, he became chairman of the Mobilization to End the War, or "Mobe" as it was known. Rennie Davis was born in 1940, attended Oberlin College, and went into radical politics as a member of SDS. Hayden recalled that Davis "peered at you from behind thick glasses with a winning, almost excessive smile, his bright white teeth gleaming even more than his blue eyes." Davis was the organizer of the group who could turn Hayden's "raw visions into concrete achievements."

The media often took the radical left at face value and depicted it as organized and cohesive. By August 1968 the reality was quite different. The events of the spring, including the demonstrations at Columbia University, had produced factional splits and in some instances a willingness to use violence to achieve goals. Tom Hayden believed it was "time to risk our necks to take democracy back, a time no longer for visionary platforms but for suffering and physical courage." At press conferences on June 29 the Mobe leaders declared that demonstrations were planned for Chicago, and in the event of violence "we will physically protect our people and are already working on chemical deterrents."

Faced with what they saw as imminent threats to the

convention and public order, Chicago authorities and the Johnson administration prepared to protect the city from the anticipated throngs of demonstrators. Having lobbied hard to persuade the Democrats to meet in his city, Mayor Daley intended to take all precautions necessary to ensure that disruptions did not mar the occasion. Daley had been a major figure in Democratic politics since delivering the state of Illinois in 1960 and helping to put John Kennedy in the White House. Presiding over "the city that works," he had been mayor for thirteen years. His roots went deep into the city's Democratic machine, and his mastery of the city faced no serious challenge. He and Lyndon Johnson cooperated for their mutual benefit. When the issue of demonstrations came up at his press conferences, the mayor told reporters, "No thousands will come to our city and take over our streets, our city, and our Convention."

To block such an event, city and federal authorities had been following the activities of radical groups through surveillance, intelligence gathering, and secret informants during the spring of 1968. The Federal Bureau of Investigation mobilized its agents to weaken the left through a variety of tactics which included anonymous letters criticizing its leaders, misinformation spread to the press, and other acts of covert disruption.

When demonstration leaders asked for city permits to allow their protests during the convention and to sleep in the city's parks, Chicago authorities spent several months in lengthy negotiations, finally refusing to sanction any rallies or marches. With the prospects of a confrontation in the air if large numbers of protesters appeared, many on the left decided not to go to Chicago. A few thousand eventually showed up from around the country, and about as many came from the immediate vicinity of the city.

Mayor Daley and the Johnson administration prepared for the worst eventualities at Chicago. The police could put twelve thousand men on the streets, and six thousand Illinois national guard troops were also assigned to duty for the convention. One thousand Secret Service men were also in attendance. The FBI added another group of its agents, and private security guards were available as well. As a result, security at the convention was extraordinary. Delegates had to present special identification cards to gain entrance to the International Amphitheatre where the proceedings were held. Around the convention hall were fences and barbed wire. Outside the city were federal troops ready to put down any evidence of civil disobedience and violence. The atmosphere of an armed camp foreshadowed the violence that would make the convention so damaging to the Democratic party.

Violence began as the convention opened. On August 26 police used tear gas to force demonstrators out of Lincoln Park on the city's North Side, in observance of an 11 p.m. curfew. Officers pursued fleeing protesters as they ran from the park. The next night the scene was repeated. At an evening rally Jerry Rubin said, "If they try to keep us out of the park, then we'll go to the streets. They bring out the pigs to protect the pigs they nominate." After leaving Lincoln Park the protesters moved to Grant Park, near the city's Loop, where they stayed through the evening. During the afternoon of Wednesday, August 28, violence occurred at a rally in Grant Park that had been approved by city authorities. When a demonstrator appeared to be taking down a flag near the bandshell where the rally was being held, police moved in and clubbed some of those present. The crowd responded by throwing bricks, pieces of concrete, and food at the policemen. Demonstrators shouted, "Death to the pigs" and "Fascist bastards." British reporters in the crowd later wrote that the police "went, quite literally, berserk."

Inside the convention hall the Democrats were tearing themselves apart. The crucial debate on the peace plank about Vietnam occurred that Wednesday afternoon. It was relatively muted as both sides recognized that the outcome was a foregone conclusion. The antiwar forces did succeed in having the debate moved back to late afternoon, but that was their only victory of the day. The administration controlled the debate, arguing that a bombing halt would imperil the lives of American soldiers in the field. A Humphrey spokesman announced to the convention that "the Vice President fully supports the majority plank." The vote was decisive in favor of the Johnson position, 1,567 votes in favor, 1,041 against. Peace advocates prayed and sang "We Shall Overcome." Others chanted, "Stop the war, stop the war!"

That evening the nominating process began. As it went forward, the most serious outbreak of rioting also erupted. It began at about eight o'clock and lasted for half an hour. Some three thousand Mobilization demonstrators and others were congregated near the Conrad Hilton Hotel on South Michigan Avenue. As the police attempted to prevent a march, many officers charged the crowd. A British correspondent recorded, "The kids screamed and were beaten to the ground by cops who had completely lost their cool." Some of the policemen chanted, "Kill, kill." In the confrontation, spectators were driven through plate glass windows at the Hilton. During thirty minutes of violence the smell of tear gas permeated the area and the blood of those whom the police had beaten was everywhere. The events were well covered by national television reporters who began to prepare their footage for broadcast later that evening. Foreign journalists, who had experience with the violent ways of police forces in their own countries, spoke later of the "ferocity" with which the Chicago police responded to events.

While the violence was happening, and as news of the events made its way into the convention hall, the ritual of nominating a presidential candidate had begun. Humphrey's name had been placed in nomination and a seconding speech was about to start when the networks were ready to air their coverage of the rioting. For almost twenty minutes the convention was forgotten and television viewers saw what was happening in the streets. The impact on the Democratic party was indelible. Here was abundant evidence that lawlessness seemed to accompany Democratic politicians and their policies.

The climax of the evening came when Senator Abraham Ribicoff of Connecticut, nominating George McGovern, denounced "Gestapo tactics on the streets of Chicago." The watching Mayor Daley, sitting only a few feet from the podium, shouted a crude, anti-Semitic remark to the senator. Ribicoff replied, "How hard it is to accept the truth." The rest of the balloting went forward later in the evening. Humphrey was nominated with 1,760¼ votes to 601 for McCarthy, 146½ for McGovern, and the remainder scattered among other candidates. When a television picture of Mrs. Humphrey was shown in the candidate's hotel suite, the vice president exuberantly kissed the screen in his happiness.

Humphrey had the nomination he had pursued for so long, but its value to him at the moment was dubious. The convention had left the Democrats torn into discordant factions and with an accurate popular perception that they could not keep their own house in order. For Richard Nixon, watching in Key Biscayne, Florida, "it seemed as if the Democrats' convention was confirming every indictment of their leadership that I had made in my campaign speeches."

The events in the streets of Chicago produced two public reactions. For many liberal Democrats and for the radical antiwar forces, the actions of the Chicago police were convincing evidence of the bankruptcy of the American political system. As the police moved in, those fleeing them cried out, "The whole world is watching." The protesters seemed confident that the American public would sympathize with their treatment by Mayor Daley's cops. They soon found out how mistaken they were.

Polls taken soon after the convention showed that more than 71 percent of those surveyed supported the measures Mayor Daley had taken to maintain security. Fifty-six percent agreed with the way he had handled the disorders themselves. Defenders of the Chicago police emphasized the demonstrators' threats and provocations. "Those police took a lot of brutality from that mob, and they did their duty," said Senator Russell Long of Louisiana. The *Indianapolis News* concluded that "the demonstrators were in many cases openly violating the law, and in general seeking the trouble they got." Mayor Daley put out his own televised broadcast giving his interpretation of what happened. In the public relations battle, the mayor of Chicago and his police force were the clear winners in August 1968.

A federal investigating commission later decided that a "police riot" had occurred, a verdict that became accepted in the years that followed. The main figures among the organizers of the Chicago protest, Hayden, Rubin, Hoffman, Dellinger, Davis, and several others, were indicted on a charge of conspiracy to riot, and a celebrated trial of the "Chicago Seven" ended in convictions for some that an appeals court later overturned.

Hubert Humphrey recognized that the events in Chicago had been a "catastrophe" for his presidential aspirations. He had two opportunities to repair some of the damage to his candidacy before the convention adjourned. The choice of a vice president would indicate his priorities as a leader and his electoral strategy. And his acceptance speech gave him an opportunity to reach out to his defeated rivals and to put some symbolic distance between himself and Lyndon Johnson.

Humphrey's choice for vice president was Senator Edmund Muskie of Maine. He had attractive qualities. A Catholic of Polish background, he would offset some of the perceived appeal of Spiro Agnew to ethnic voters. Much quieter than Humphrey, Muskie seemed a solid contrast to the voluble and excitable vice president. Humphrey thought it was necessary to have "a competent able man who could do a good job as President" rather than "some kind of compromise for geography or ideology."

These were laudable sentiments, but Humphrey was acting as if he had already won the election rather than facing a campaign in which he was the clear underdog. It is hard to see what Muskie brought to the ticket in electoral terms. He helped to carry his own state in the fall, but Maine's four electoral votes were scarcely crucial. Muskie's selection did not address those areas in which the Democrats were weak in 1968—in the border states and the South, in California, or west of the Mississippi River. The selection of a Southern governor such as Terry Sanford of North Carolina or Senator Fred Harris of Oklahoma would have been a sign that Humphrey was not conceding any section of the country to his opponents. Instead the Democratic ticket now had two Northern liberals from small states. The choice of Muskie won plaudits from editorial writers. It did not show Humphrey as a politician who was playing to win this crucial election.

Humphrey's aides urged him to use his acceptance speech for a dramatic gesture that would emphasize his disagreement with Lyndon Johnson. They suggested that he resign as vice president and thereby declare his independence from the administration. When his advisers persuaded Larry O'Brien to lay the idea before Humphrey on August 28, he turned it down as "a gimmick." In a more telling appraisal of his continuing fear of Lyndon Johnson, he added, "And it will enrage the president."

Containing no surprises and no divergence from the policies of the Johnson administration, the acceptance speech was a sound example of political oratory but not the transforming moment needed by Humphrey's faltering campaign. He praised Johnson for having "accomplished more of the unfinished business of America than any of his modern predecessors." He promised he would try "to bring a prompt end" to the war in Vietnam. He denounced crime because "neither mob violence nor police brutality have any place in America." Toward the end of the speech he called on McCarthy and McGovern for help "in the difficult campaign that lies ahead."

Having identified himself with the Johnson administration, Humphrey was not about to repudiate the president's policies. He offered no recognition of the sincere and legitimate protest mounted by McCarthy and his followers. It might not have mattered. As he would during most of the fall campaign, McCarthy was staying aloof from Humphrey and his election. In a speech to his followers in Grant Park the afternoon following Humphrey's selection, McCarthy referred to "the government of the people in exile." McCarthy's manner toward Humphrey was infuriating to the candidate, especially his refusal to appear on the podium when Humphrey accepted the nomination. Deferential toward Lyndon Johnson, Humphrey felt less sympathy toward the disaffected wing of the Democratic party.

Humphrey's public comments about the violence of the Chicago police added to the anger of liberal Democrats toward his candidacy. In a television interview, Humphrey said, "We ought to quit pretending that Mayor Daley did anything wrong. He didn't...." When disturbances between protesters and police continued on Thursday, August 29, and into Friday, including a late-night raid against McCarthy's headquarters in the Conrad Hilton, the vice president was asked to intercede to stop the attacks. His press secretary declined to awaken him. The incident enraged McCarthy and helps to explain his unwillingness to endorse Humphrey that fall. In a 1971 interview, Humphrey said his experience with protesters during his campaign disposed him to think, "Well, they're just not decent people."

The Democrats left Chicago with their party in a shambles. The rioting in the streets had associated them in the minds of many Americans with lawlessness and disorder, precisely the charges leveled against them by Richard Nixon and George Wallace. Under the impact of the Vietnam War and the race issue, Democratic party machinery could not contain the deep divisions opened up during Lyndon Johnson's presidency. Among Democrats, resentments formed at Chicago persisted for years. While the rules changes that came out of the convention eliminated some of the inequities that had led to Humphrey's nomination, the unintended consequences of such reforms proved as disastrous as the earlier weaknesses they had sought to correct.

As the traditional Labor Day campaign opening neared in September 1968, the three contenders for the presidency began the race in very different conditions. Nixon was well rested and confident after a harmonious convention and a chance to court the various factions within his party. Wallace would not be formally nominated until mid-September when the American Independent party gathered in Dallas to make the obvious choice official. Polls indicated how well both Nixon and Wallace were doing. A Gallup survey after the Democratic convention showed that 43 percent of the electorate preferred Nixon, 30 percent was for Humphrey, and 19 percent for Wallace, with only 7 percent still undecided. During the remainder of September, Humphrey's support fell away and Nixon opened up a lead of 43 percent to 28 percent by late in the month. Some Republicans began talking of a landslide victory.

Humphrey's campaign, on the other hand, was feeble in every respect. Trailing in the polls, his money dried up in a period before presidential candidates received federal matching funds. The vice president attempted to tap into some of the money that Lyndon Johnson had raised for the Democrats, but the president made it clear that neither he nor his fund-raisers would be at Humphrey's disposal. Despite vigorous courting of Johnson in early September, the vice president gained access to none of the president's financial resources. He was forced to borrow money to fund his campaign advertising. Meanwhile, disorganization characterized the Humphrey campaign. Lawrence O'Brien, Orville Freeman (the secretary of agriculture), Walter Mondale, and Fred Harris vied with other Humphrey insiders for control of the campaign. Worst of all, there was no overall campaign plan until a political consultant named Joe Napolitan hammered out a rough blueprint in mid-September. He urged Humphrey to separate himself from Johnson on Vietnam and to point out his differences from Nixon on the issue of crime and justice. These were themes that might structure a Humphrey rebound, but they were not yet in place while the campaign struggled during September.

Richard Nixon started his campaign with electoral assets that made his task much easier. During the 1950s and 1960s a Republican electoral "lock" had begun to fall into place that put certain states in the GOP column no matter whom the Democrats nominated. Nixon had at least 110 to 120 electoral votes from Indiana, Utah, Wyoming, Colorado, Oklahoma, Kansas, and other states that could not be wrested from him regardless of Democratic effort. Reflecting a shrewd appraisal of Republican chances for electoral votes, the Nixon campaign selected fourteen states with 298 electoral votes as prime targets. Among these were California with 40 electoral votes, Illinois with 26 votes, Michigan with 21, and Texas with 25. Beyond that, Nixon hoped to contest Wallace in the border states of the South and a few Deep South bastions such as South Carolina. The central point of the Republicans' advantage in 1968 was that it allowed them to pick their states of opportunity and use their extensive financial and campaign resources most effectively. Democrats, on the other hand, could count almost no states where victory was certain. Had George Wallace not been in the race as a third-party candidate, the Republican margin over Humphrey would have been decisive, since most of the Wallace vote either would have gone to Nixon or would have stayed home in November.

During September George Wallace's campaign seemed to be gathering momentum. He gained three percentage points in the public opinion polls during September and stood at 21 percent of the vote in a three-way contest as the month ended. His campaign style seemed as effective in the fall as it had been in the spring. He could reasonably expect to carry enough of the South to force the election into the House of Representatives. This electoral potential made Wallace an important element in the 1968 race, both for the issues he raised and for his effect on the major party candidates. The central theme of his campaign remained the issue of law and order. "Anarchists better have their day now," he told a California audience, "because after Nov. 5, you're through." He denounced the federal government for money spent to "trifle with my child's education." He pledged to return to the people "absolute control of public schools." On the issue of urban violence, he declared, "We gonna have a police state for folks who burn the cities down. They aren't gonna burn any more cities."

To the dismay of Democratic leaders who were counting on a large union vote for Humphrey, Wallace seemed to be having a serious impact on labor support outside the South.

As Humphrey recognized, Wallace was making an appeal in which " 'crime' and 'black' got tied together, so that every threat" to the union members' "property or persons appeared to be a black threat." A United Auto Workers official in New Jersey summed up the essence of Wallace's allure for Northern union men: "The men in the plants want to zap the Negroes by voting for Wallace."

Wallace was scornful of both Democrats and Republicans. "If you can show me one thing the national Republican party has ever done for the average citizen of Texas or Alabama, I'll get out of the race for the Presidency, because you can't show me one thing they've ever done." To one audience he proclaimed, "You get a bayonet in your back with the national Democrats and you get a bayonet in your back with the national Republicans." He charged that "the average American is sick and tired of all these over-educated, ivory-tower folks with pointed heads looking down their noses at us, and the left-wing liberal press writing editorials and guidelines."

For a moment Wallace seemed to be unstoppable. Hecklers plagued his rallies, but he used them as foils to whip his crowds to even greater enthusiasm and support. David Broder of the *Washington Post* observed that he had not seen a candidate "who communicates so clearly to his crowd— whose humor, whose warnings, whose admonitions and whose predictions draw the response that Wallace's do." Despite attacks on the Wallace sentiment as "an evil phenomenon" and the basis for a fascist movement, the Alabama governor had the national political establishment scared.

The start of Richard Nixon's campaign was also promising. With ample money to spend, especially compared with Humphrey's poverty, the candidate did not have to devote time to fund-raising. A highly professional organization managed Nixon's time to the best effect, and he appeared in events that showed his abilities to the voters in the most attractive settings. Where Humphrey and Wallace had to deal with persistent hecklers, the Nixon campaign was able to exclude people who might disturb his rallies.

He began his campaign in Chicago, and the 400,000 people who turned out offered a striking contrast to what the Democrats had experienced in the city just a week earlier. The crowds remained large and friendly during the weeks that followed. He had worked out his standard campaign speech which he delivered with practiced expertise. He brushed aside Humphrey's calls for a debate and pitched his appeal to the "Forgotten Americans, those who did not indulge in violence, those who did not break the law, people who pay their taxes and go to work, people who send their children to school, who go to their churches, people who are not haters, people who love this country."

On Vietnam, Nixon reiterated the position he had adopted since the beginning of the year. If the war continued on November 5, he told crowds, "if after all the power and the support the Administration has had, then they've had their chance, now give us our chance. We will end the war on an honorable basis." For young people angry at the draft, he promised, once "our involvement in the Vietnam war is behind us," to "move toward an all-volunteer armed force."

His stance on civil rights was designed to position him between Humphrey and Wallace in a way that appealed to Southern voters. He endorsed the decision in *Brown v. Board of Education* but quickly added that the federal government should not interfere with local school districts or use "the power of the Federal Treasury to withhold funds or give funds" in order to promote desegregation. He described efforts to transport children from slum areas to wealthier schools as futile. "They are two or three grades behind, and all you do is to destroy their ability to compete." When asked to appear in black districts, he declined. "I am not going to campaign for the black vote at the risk of alienating the suburban vote." His attitude toward black voters was stark. "If I am President, I am not going to owe anything to the black community."

The Nixon campaign presented its candidate to television viewers with a media skill that would be the trademark of Republican campaigns for two decades to follow. Nixon himself was not comfortable in unscripted settings, and he did not project himself well on television, as his debates with John F. Kennedy in 1960 had showed. Given the proper context, however, Nixon could appear to good advantage. As one of his media advisers observed, "He should be presented in some kind of 'situation' rather than cold in a studio. The situation should look unstaged even if it is not."

His advisers used the format of Nixon as "the man in the arena" which had worked so well during the primary campaign. He appeared in regional broadcasts which drew larger audiences than ordinary political shows. Campaign commercials struck the major themes of the Nixon appeal. One showed a woman moving down a dark street while the announcer intoned, "Crimes of violence in the United States have almost doubled in recent years." Another featured scenes of urban rioting with Nixon saying, "We see cities enveloped in smoke and flame. We hear sirens in the night. As we see and hear these things, millions of Americans cry out in anguish. Did we come all the way for this?"

The combined efforts of the Nixon and Wallace campaigns put the Democrats on the defensive at the opening of the 1968 campaign. In the first weeks of September the Humphrey camp was suffused with an atmosphere of defeat. Yet by the end of the month the vice president's campaign had regained momentum, and the race tightened dramatically. President Johnson's diplomacy toward Vietnam also helped Humphrey throughout October. From the possible rout of the Democrats that seemed likely after the Chicago convention, the 1968 presidential election became a matter of suspense and surprises.

6

October Surprises

IN THE AFTERMATH of the Chicago convention, a revival of Hubert Humphrey's fortunes seemed highly improbable. Almost everything that could go wrong with a campaign did so as Humphrey struggled to find his message and to appeal effectively to voters.

Faced with an almost hopeless situation, Democrats decided to concentrate on their traditional base of support. They saw no possibility of carrying the South or most of the border states against either Wallace or Nixon. Because of President Johnson, they did not entirely write off Texas. Humphrey hoped to run strongly in the Northeast and win California, Michigan, Illinois, and New Jersey. The aim of the Humphrey campaign was to emphasize that the choice lay between himself and Nixon, and in that way persuade liberal Democrats and moderate Republicans to pick him as the only sensible alternative to Nixon or Wallace.

First, Humphrey had to revive his own campaign, and that proved difficult during September. His initial appearances attracted disappointing crowds, and hecklers dogged him everywhere. As long as he was perceived as a loser, campaign funds failed to come in. His managers had to go into debt to put television commercials on the air during the last weeks of the campaign. Democrats avoided him when he visited their states or cities.

Eugene McCarthy turned back all of Humphrey's pleas for assistance. Still angry over what had happened in Chicago, and seeing Humphrey as identified with Johnson's policies on the war, McCarthy kept himself aloof from the Democratic candidate. He traveled in Europe for a month, then covered the World Series for *Life* magazine. One of Humphrey's friends complained angrily that McCarthy was "a slick political parasite—he always gives less than he receives, and is mean as hell to boot." McCarthy's failure to endorse Humphrey, and his obvious disdain for his old friend, hurt the vice president among liberals.

Humphrey's overriding problem remained Lyndon Johnson and the Vietnam War. No matter how Humphrey tried to put some daylight between Johnson and himself, the president would not give him any. When his campaign opened in Philadelphia on September 9 Humphrey said he hoped to be able to remove some troops from Vietnam within a few months after the election. He also had kind words for the defeated minority plank at the Chicago convention. Misreading a newspaper story, Humphrey even once again declared that American troops would be coming home—he failed to notice that it was only a routine replacement of one unit by another.

An obviously irritated Johnson wasted little time in rebuking Humphrey. The Defense Department repudiated what Humphrey had announced. Even more wounding was the statement of the president himself. Speaking to the American Legion convention in New Orleans the following day, Johnson said, "We yearn for the day when our men can come home. No man can predict when that day will come, because we are there to bring an honorable, stable peace to Southeast Asia, and no less will justify the sacrifices that our men have died for." Humphrey would later ask himself, "I wonder why Johnson shot me down." Once again, the president "made me look like a damned fool, and I never fully recovered from it."

Johnson's motives toward Humphrey during the first half of the campaign probably reflected his stroking by Nixon, so skillfully accomplished throughout 1968. The president also resented the efforts of people around Humphrey to separate their candidate from an unpopular president. Whenever Humphrey put one of his own people in a party leadership position, Johnson took it as a rebuke. Johnson told Clark Clifford he doubted whether "Humphrey had the ability to be President." He was disappointed that Humphrey had not "showed he had some balls."

Adding to Johnson's frustration were the gloomy prospects for his handpicked nominee for chief justice. During September, critics of the Abe Fortas nomination had complained about the money that the justice received for teaching at American University during the summers and his role in advising President Johnson about policy matters and in speech writing. Support for the nomination had begun to erode. When the issue went to the Senate on September 25, the Republicans began a filibuster. Prospects for Fortas's confirmation seemed bleak once the minority leader, Everett Dirksen of Illinois, indicated he would not vote for cloture to cut off the filibuster.

Defeat for Johnson came a few days later. On October 1 the Democratic leader, Mike Mansfield of Montana, tried to break the Republican filibuster. Needing two-thirds of the Senate to shut off the extended debate, the pro-Fortas senators could achieve a majority of only 45 to 43, fourteen votes short of what was needed. The Fortas nomination was dead, as the justice and the president both recognized. The choice of the next chief justice would be left to the winner of the presidential race.

By late September the men around Humphrey told him he must loosen his ties to Johnson on the Vietnam War. At one point he told a friend, "I think I've had Lyndon Johnson around my neck just long enough." But making a formal break proved to be difficult. A nationwide speech was scheduled for Monday, September 30, when Humphrey would be in Salt Lake City. His problem was to distance himself from Johnson on the war without provoking a devastating response from the White House.

In the days that preceded the broadcast, tensions mounted within the Humphrey camp as advisers battled over the language of the speech. Polls showed Humphrey fifteen percentage points behind Nixon, and fund-raising remained slow. In speeches the Democratic candidate was subjected to intense heckling and booing. Clearly he could not go on as he had been doing throughout September. But how far should he move in separating himself from Johnson?

After many drafts and much squabbling about the contents of the speech, the candidate hammered out an acceptable version almost at the last minute. He called Johnson and laid out what he was going to say. Johnson responded, "I gather you're not asking my advice." The language in the speech as delivered was cautious. "As President," Humphrey said, "I would stop the bombing of the North as an acceptable risk for peace because I believe it could lead to success in the negotiations and thereby shorten the war." He carefully added that in making any decision he would take into account evidence of how the communists would respond. "If the Government of North Vietnam were to show bad faith, I would reserve the right to resume the bombing."

One of Johnson's aides described Humphrey's statement as "fuzzy and ambiguous." So it was, but its tone was far more conciliatory to the antiwar wing of the Democrats than anything the administration had offered at the Chicago convention or during the weeks that followed. The public reaction was quite positive for Humphrey's campaign. His men told the press, "What he's really saying is that he'd pull the troops out and try to end the war January the twenty-first, 1969." Headlines indicated that he would stop the bombing, and signs appeared at Humphrey's rallies that said, "If You Mean It, We're with You."

Nixon responded coolly to Humphrey's speech. "Humphrey either has to be for the bombing halt," said the Republican candidate, "or he has to support the negotiations in Paris." Nixon was unsure "which side he is on." In fact, Nixon knew that the prospect of peace in Vietnam might undercut all his careful planning to achieve the presidency. He was aware that Johnson's announcement of an imminent peace would be "the one move that I thought could determine the outcome of the election."

The Nixon campaign had reached a high degree of optimism during the early weeks of September. With crowds so friendly, the campaign organization working smoothly, and the Humphrey campaign apparently collapsing because of its own inner problems, the men around Nixon thought for a time of such unlikely feats as carrying New York for the Republicans. A decisive victory for Nixon seemed certain.

Two areas of concern persisted. The vice-presidential candidate had proved more of a weakness than a strength for the ticket. Unskilled in national politics, Spiro Agnew had a flair for inept statements. He called Humphrey "soft on Communism," a phrase that revived memories of Senator

Joseph R. McCarthy during the 1950s. Agnew referred to ethnic groups in demeaning terms. When asked why he did not travel through ghetto areas, he replied, "When you've seen one slum, you've seen them all." These comments did not hurt Agnew in the border states and the South, where Nixon was focusing his appeal, but they embarrassed Republicans in the Northeast. The Nixon campaign kept Agnew under closer supervision; Nixon rarely mentioned the name of his running mate.

The second problem was more serious. Despite Nixon's lengthening lead over Humphrey, most of his gain had come because the vice president had dropped in the polls. Nixon's own percentage of the vote remained fixed at around 40 percent. One Republican analyst, Walter DeVries, noted this trend and worried that Nixon might not be able to push his numbers above the 40 percent range as long as Wallace remained a candidate. "This race is by no means in the bag for Nixon," he wrote. A Nixon aide and future columnist, William Safire, remembered that by early October "Humphrey was beginning to move up in our own private polls; organized labor was doing its job of winning back union members to the Democratic fold, and the erosion of the Wallace strength was going Humphrey's way and not ours."

Wallace's candidacy had slipped during the early days of October. The choice of a vice-presidential candidate hurt him. After considering several conservative figures, Wallace selected a retired air force general, Curtis E. LeMay. A veteran of the bombing campaigns against Germany and Japan during World War II, LeMay had led the Strategic Air Command during the 1950s and then served as air force chief of staff until he retired in 1965. He had suggested the United States tell North Vietnam "to draw in their horns and stop their aggression or we're going to bomb them back into the Stone Age."

The introduction of LeMay to the press on October 3 was a fiasco. The general defended the use of nuclear bombs and observed, "I don't believe the world will end if we explode a nuclear weapon." Wallace tried vainly to soften the impact of LeMay's remarks, but the damage had been done. LeMay was also a poor speaker who added little to the Wallace campaign. Placards appeared at Wallace rallies protesting the vice-presidential choice: "Bombs Away with Curt Le-May." Within days of his announcement, LeMay was telling friends he was "fed up to his teeth" about getting into the presidential campaign.

Another problem for Wallace was organized labor's campaign against him. The AFL-CIO told their members in the North that Wallace had backed antilabor legislation in Alabama. In addition, his state lacked adequate child-labor laws, had no minimum-wage provisions, and was stingy with welfare payments. Against these bread-and-butter considerations, Wallace's racial appeal lost ground in the North. Wives of union men did not follow their husbands into the Wallace fold. As a result, the union vote returned to the Democrats in key Northern states.

Wallace soon slipped in the polls. His total fell from a high of 21 percent in late September to 13 percent by the end of October. The disorder at Wallace rallies, and physical attacks by his supporters against protesters, mocked the candidate's claims to be a champion of law and order. As the election neared, voters decided that Nixon or Humphrey would soon be president and Wallace would not. One voter summed it up well: "Hell, a vote for him is wasted."

Wallace also faced pressure from Republicans. Led by

Strom Thurmond, GOP campaigners told Southerners that a vote for Wallace helped only the "unacceptable Hubert Humphrey." Spiro Agnew echoed this theme to Southern audiences. "Wallace is dangerous because he is not electable," he said in Charleston, South Carolina, in September. "He will divide the vote." For the most part, Nixon ignored Wallace. On one of the few occasions when he referred to the Alabama governor, Nixon admitted he shared some of Wallace's frustrations about "the rise in crime, the conduct of our foreign policy, what's happened to American respect around the world.... I'm against a lot of these things.... The difference is I'm for a lot of things, and that's what we need now." In the last weeks of the campaign Nixon made impressive inroads into Wallace support in the South.

Both of the major party candidates adopted some of Wallace's law-and-order themes. Nixon stressed the issue from the opening of the campaign. In Dallas on October 11 he again promised "a new Attorney General who will launch an all-out battle against organized crime and guarantee the first civil right of every American—the right to be free from domestic violence." In a televised interview about urban riots, Humphrey assured viewers that "as President I would stop these outrages at whatever cost."

When Wallace stalled, the Nixon camp felt the race tightening. To some degree the Republicans had overestimated their chances and had begun to act as if Nixon could not lose. They had an overwhelming advantage in their ability to dominate the media phase of the campaign. Republican commercials were better produced and more sharply focused. The party was unified behind Nixon. Though the Republican candidate and his men intensified their attacks on Humphrey as the campaign neared its end, Nixon followed his strategy of limited public appearances and controlled exposure to the press.

Republican overconfidence became a drawback. Nixon ran to protect his lead in the polls rather than to expand it. "We set out trying to save what we had, short of boredom," a party operative said after the election. When pressed, Nixon returned to the law-and-order themes he had earlier pursued. In Ohio he charged that Humphrey was "a do-nothing candidate on law and order" who had watched the United States "become a nation where 50 per cent of American women are frightened to walk within a mile of their homes at night." These themes, and the Republican advantage in electoral votes, were designed to keep Nixon ahead until election day.

Hubert Humphrey mounted a final effort to save his candidacy and the Democrats during October. He did it in the face of formidable obstacles. Despite increased campaign contributions following his Salt Lake City speech, Democrats still lagged well behind Republicans in funds needed to pay for television time. Humphrey challenged Nixon to debate him on national television. Remembering what had happened when he debated John F. Kennedy in 1960, Nixon was "determined not to be lured into a confrontation, since Humphrey was still far behind me in the polls, and would be the beneficiary of any debate." Staging the debate would have required congressional action to modify existing equal-time regulations, and Republicans on Capitol Hill blocked legislation to that end. All Humphrey could do was to denounce "Richard the Chicken-Hearted" and "Richard the Silent."

Humphrey's problems with Lyndon Johnson also persisted. The Salt Lake City speech had irritated the president. He told James Rowe, who had again asked him to campaign for Humphrey, "I'm not sure I'll do that; Nixon is more for my policies than Humphrey." By October 10 Johnson came around to a public endorsement of the Democratic ticket in a radio broadcast. The president denounced "the Nixon-Agnew Republican record of reaction and recession" and urged support "for progressive Democratic leadership in America." Johnson also asked his wealthy friends to contribute to Humphrey's campaign.

Eugene McCarthy was not that forgiving. The Minnesota senator told New York Democrats on October 8 that he had run "to test the unity of the party on what we considered to be vital matters. I see no reason why if the cry for unity then was not acceptable, it is any more acceptable today." McCarthy argued that the Democrats should halt the bombing of North Vietnam unconditionally, accept free elections in South Vietnam, reform American draft laws, and reshape their party. Until these changes occurred, McCarthy said, he had no time for the Humphrey campaign.

On October 11 the political situation shifted dramatically in favor of Humphrey and the Democrats. Negotiations between the United States and North Vietnam in Paris, which had begun after Johnson's withdrawal statement of March 31, had been deadlocked. The president insisted that any further halt in the bombing campaign in North Vietnam must have an acceptable response from Hanoi. Such an answer would include a willingness to include the South Vietnamese government in subsequent talks about peace. Until October 11 Hanoi had insisted on a complete end to the bombing of their country and opposed any South Vietnamese participation in peace negotiations. On that date, however, they indicated to the American representatives in Paris, Cyrus Vance and Averell Harriman, that upon a cessation of the bombing Hanoi would agree to accept South Vietnamese delegates to the talks.

Johnson and his aides knew it was probably too late in his presidency to achieve an end to the war in Vietnam, but getting negotiations under way would be a significant step toward a conclusion to the fighting. Any movement toward peace would also help Humphrey. To what extent, then, did Lyndon Johnson consider a peace initiative in October 1968 as a means of helping Humphrey and the Democrats win the White House? In part, the opportunity for such an initiative arose because, after Humphrey's Salt Lake City speech, the North Vietnamese probably concluded that the Democratic candidate was more likely to end the war than was Richard Nixon. So the chance to push for negotiations came to Johnson more because of what Humphrey had done than because of White House action.

Once the break in the diplomatic situation occurred, however, political considerations inevitably arose. During the extended deliberations that followed at the White House, Lyndon Johnson said, according to notes preserved by an aide, "They think everybody is working toward electing Humphrey by doing this. This is not what motivates us." On the other hand, Johnson had told Humphrey in August that he would offer the vice president a better chance for peace than any speech Humphrey could make. In Johnson's mind, his primary goal was the peace process, with Humphrey's election a happy by-product.

The Nixon camp, however, feared the president's actions might snatch away an electoral victory that was all but won. On October 12 Richard Nixon received word from Henry Kissinger "that there was a strong possibility that the administration would move before October 23." A Harvard professor and adviser to Nelson Rockefeller, Kissinger had taken part in diplomatic negotiations about Vietnam for the Johnson administration in 1967. He had begun offering cautious advice to the Nixon camp in September 1968. At one point in late September or early October, Kissinger warned Nixon "about the moves Johnson may take." He predicted that Johnson "will take some action before the election." So Nixon was disposed to weigh Kissinger's words seriously.

For five days after the break in the talks at Paris, the White House sought to confirm various aspects of the proposed agreement with all parties involved. The key point was the willingness of the South Vietnamese to come to the peace table before election day. Their situation was the exact opposite of their military enemies. Humphrey's September 30 statement seemed likely to make him less sympathetic to Saigon's view of the war once he became president. Nixon's election, on the other hand, would give South Vietnam a president more favorable to its view. So President Thieu of South Vietnam had no incentive to agree to peace talks before election day. In effect, Saigon held an implicit veto over Johnson's peace plan. Thieu could not exercise it publicly, but he was a clever man who knew how to use the machinery of his government for purposes of delay and caution.

A lengthy series of meetings at the White House on October 14 produced new instructions to the Paris negotiators to go forward with talks aimed at a bombing halt and peace negotiations. They contained a significant new condition: Hanoi must open discussions within twenty-four hours after the bombing stopped. At one point, according to Johnson, his friends said, "The word is out that we are making an effort to throw the election to Humphrey." The next day both Hanoi and Saigon were delaying their responses to the Johnson instructions. The condition of meeting within twenty-four hours was modified. It became a date to be set only after the bombing ceased.

On October 16 the president held a telephone conference call with all three presidential candidates to bring them up to date on the status of the peace initiative. He told them he was requiring Hanoi to open talks after the bombing stopped and to limit hostilities against South Vietnam. That evening, at the dinner of the Alfred E. Smith Foundation in New York City, Johnson gently jabbed at Nixon in his "nonpartisan" remarks. "Pretty soon," he told the audience, "you won't have Lyndon Johnson to kick around any more." Privately he asked Nixon to "be careful" about what he had to say on Vietnam. The next day Nixon offered public support to a possible bombing halt because "We do not want to play politics with peace."

During the following week, rumors of an imminent deal with North Vietnam circulated internationally. In South Vietnam, President Thieu pressed the United States not to allow representatives of the National Liberation Front (NLF), the communists in South Vietnam, to take part in the peace talks. By October 21 Thieu was telling the American ambassador that the NLF should be at the Paris discussions only as part of the larger North Vietnamese delegation. Saigon's new demand was not likely to please Hanoi. In the United States, meanwhile, Humphrey gained on Nixon as the election neared. By October 24 Nixon's lead had shrunk to eight percentage points, with 44 percent for the Republicans, 36 percent for Humphrey, and Wallace down to 15 percent.

With the election in the balance, behind-the-scenes politics became intense and dirty. Neither Lyndon Johnson nor Richard Nixon held back any of the weapons at his command. Nixon's careful planning and shrewd sense of partisan infighting gave him a decided edge. Through a Republican associate named Bryce Harlow, who had excellent contacts in the government, Nixon had a "double agent" in the Johnson White House. As Harlow later put it, "I knew about every meeting they held. I knew who attended the meetings. I knew what their next move was going to be."

In his memoirs Nixon described Harlow's source as "someone in Johnson's innermost circle." That judgment was probably an exaggeration. Harlow's information could have been gleaned from a member of the clerical staff. In one case the agent mistakenly said that White House aide Joseph Califano was attending the foreign policy meetings when in fact he was not. In any event, the information convinced Nixon that Johnson was seeking a bombing halt in order to aid Humphrey's election. Nixon became certain on October 24 when the source told Harlow that "an agreement had been reached with the North Vietnamese the day before."

The information was premature. No agreement with either North Vietnam or South Vietnam was yet in place. The president's urgency grew as the election neared. On October 25 the Soviet Union indicated it wanted a quick solution to the diplomatic deadlock. Since the White House attached great importance to Moscow's influence with Hanoi, the president hoped to move quickly but without arousing press interest. White House efforts to keep the story under wraps fed the impression that Johnson was arranging a last-minute deal for Humphrey.

Nixon now moved publicly to forestall the president. On Saturday, October 26, he issued a statement saying there had been "a flurry of meetings" to produce "an agreement on a bombing halt accompanied possibly by a cease-fire in the immediate future." He added that he had been told it was "a cynical last-minute attempt by President Johnson to salvage the candidacy of Mr. Humphrey. This I do not believe." Nixon was turning up the heat on the president.

At the same time the Republican candidate attacked the administration's defense policies. On October 24 he charged that "the present state of our defenses is much too close to the peril point," contributing to "a gravely serious security gap." Hubert Humphrey and the White House struck back angrily at these statements. Johnson called Nixon's remarks "ugly and unfair charges," first about the nation's security position as well as "about our attempts to win peace in the world." Democrats suggested that the "Old Nixon," the politician of slashing attacks and partisan charges, had reappeared.

When he appeared on the televised news program "Face the Nation" on Sunday, October 27, Nixon responded to this dual assault on his Vietnam and national security statements. Supporting his attacks on defense policy, he cited Democratic senators who had warned about an alleged Soviet missile buildup. On the question of Vietnam he sought to align himself once again with Johnson's substantive position and to separate the president from Humphrey. "I back him up," Nixon said, "and I only wish that Hubert Humphrey now would button up his lip and stick with the President on this." Nixon assailed "White House insiders" sympathetic to Humphrey who "were attempting to work out some sort of a settlement."

At the same time he was supporting Johnson's negotiating position in public, Nixon was using another channel in an effort to stave off the bombing halt that might defeat his candidacy. Through Anna Chennault and the contacts established in the summer of 1968, the Nixon campaign encouraged the South Vietnamese government not to yield to White House pressure. On October 23, for example, the

South Vietnamese ambassador in Washington cabled Saigon: "Many Republican friends have contacted me and encouraged us to stand firm. They were alarmed by press reports to the effect that you had already softened your position." Another cable on October 29 reported that the ambassador was in touch with people around Nixon.

The National Security Agency intercepted these communications between Saigon and its Washington embassy as part of a constant monitoring of South Vietnamese diplomatic messages. Clark Clifford later described these activities as "extremely sensitive intelligence-gathering operations" in which the FBI and the Central Intelligence Agency also took part. One key passage in an October 27 cable from Washington said, "The longer the present situation continues, the more we are favored...." With these facts in hand, Johnson directed the FBI to put Anna Chennault under surveillance, including wiretapping her telephone conversations. Nixon also believed that Johnson turned wiretapping or electronic surveillance against the Nixon campaign plane.

The White House now had potentially explosive information about secret Republican negotiations with Saigon to block the peace initiative. The problem was that in revealing such information Johnson would also have to disclose *how* it had been obtained. What the White House had done was not illegal, but Mrs. Chennault was an American citizen who had identified herself with the Republicans. Surveillance might well be considered a partisan tactic. Moreover, disclosure of the Chennault-Saigon channel would reveal to South Vietnam that their codes had been broken. Also to be considered were Johnson's mixed feelings about Humphrey. Was defeating Nixon at all costs in the end what Johnson really wished to accomplish? For whatever reasons, the president decided to press for peace talks without revealing what the Republicans had done.

In the negotiations with Hanoi's representatives in Paris, October 27 proved to be another crucial date. North Vietnam proposed that the United States "stop the bombing on October 30" and agreed that representatives from the National Liberation Front would be in Paris "as early as possible." This meant within three or four days after the bombing ended. At the White House, Secretary of State Dean Rusk said, "I smell Vodka and Caviar in it. We have substantial compliance. The Soviets have moved in."

Johnson now decided to order the American military commander in South Vietnam, General Creighton Abrams, back to Washington. In a series of questions he posed in the early morning of October 29, the president asked the general if a bombing halt was worth the military risk. Then came the decisive question: "If you were President, would you do it?" Abrams responded that "I have no reservations about doing it, even though I know it is stepping into a cesspool of comment. It is the proper thing to do."

Washington had made up its mind. What would Saigon do? Within hours the Johnson administration had the response. Thieu told the Americans he could not be ready by November 2 (three days before the election) because he needed to consult with leaders of his national assembly and members of his own security council. For two days the White House endeavored to obtain Thieu's formal pledge to come to the Paris talks. In one message Johnson said that Nixon had authorized the president to tell Thieu "that any messages reaching him through any channel from Republican sources should be disregarded." The South Vietnamese president would not budge. Johnson concluded on October 30 that it was necessary to announce the bombing halt regardless. He hoped to persuade Saigon to send representatives to Paris when the talks with North Vietnam resumed on Wednesday, November 6, the day after the election. Johnson scheduled a national television address for 8 p.m. on Thursday, October 31.

Two hours before the program aired, Johnson placed another conference call to the presidential candidates to tell them what he intended to say. Richard Nixon felt "my anger and frustration welling up." Would his election be "undermined by the powers of an incumbent who had decided against seeking reelection?" In the broadcast itself Johnson used carefully phrased language. The Paris talks would take place on November 6, he announced, and the representatives of South Vietnam would be "free to participate" in them.

The immediate public reaction to the bombing halt favored Hubert Humphrey. By the time Johnson went on television, the presidential race had tightened remarkably. Late polls showed Nixon and Humphrey only a few points apart. The Lou Harris poll put the vice president ahead 43 to 40. Other signs pointed toward Humphrey. Eugene McCarthy had given him a grudging endorsement on October 29 as a man who has "a better understanding of the domestic needs and a strong will to act." Even Johnson had decided to throw his support behind Humphrey. In Texas the president had brought the feuding forces of Governor John Connally and Senator Ralph Yarborough into a temporary alliance. At a huge rally in the Astrodome in Houston on November 3 Johnson declared that Humphrey "should and must become the 37th President of the United States."

Last-minute Democratic optimism rested on fragile hopes. The electoral arithmetic still favored Nixon as the likely winner, and the Republican candidate had played his hand skillfully on the issue of the bombing halt. Knowing that Thieu would refuse to send representatives to Paris, Nixon was not surprised when the South Vietnamese president announced on November 2 that his government "deeply regrets not being able to participate in the exploratory talks." With that phrase the air went out of Johnson's peace initiative.

Nixon then used all his political skill to emphasize how the White House had failed. He told television reporters that some of his aides had concluded that Johnson had used the bombing halt for political purposes. But, said Nixon, "I do not make such a charge." When Johnson called him to complain about the Chennault maneuvers toward South Vietnam, he told the president "there was absolutely no truth in it, as far as he knew." As Bryce Harlow recalled, "Probably Johnson didn't believe it. But he probably couldn't prove it, I suppose." Nixon's link to Mrs. Chennault was Spiro Agnew, thus preserving the ability of the presidential candidate to deny knowledge of her actions. During the last weekend before the election, Nixon also had his campaign manager instruct Mrs. Chennault to say nothing further.

The full dimensions of the Republican involvement with the South Vietnamese government in 1968 are still unknown. Intelligence information obtained by the Johnson administration remains classified. Nixon's defenders accuse Lyndon Johnson of using "dirty tricks" by wiretapping and electronic surveillance of Mrs. Chennault and the Republican campaign. Democrats charge that Nixon and the Republicans played politics with national security for electoral purposes.

In fact, Richard Nixon did not have to persuade the Thieu government to stay away from Johnson's peace proposal. It was not in Saigon's interest to participate. But it is also clear that the Republican candidate sanctioned communications between his campaign and South Vietnam and thereby sought to counteract Lyndon Johnson's efforts. If the information from the Chennault channel had only a marginal impact on Thieu's decision, it was not for lack of effort on the part of Nixon and his aides. When they learned later of the White House surveillance that had occurred in 1968, they thought themselves justified in adopting similar measures when they were in power. To that extent, the Chennault episode contained some of the seeds of the Watergate scandal of the early 1970s.

With the last-minute tide of opinion swinging back to Nixon, there remained one final card for Johnson or Humphrey to play. They could have broken the story about the ties between the Nixon campaign and Anna Chennault. The problem was just what Bryce Harlow had surmised: the only proof for the story lay in the intelligence information that, were it to be revealed, would damage Johnson as much as it would hurt Nixon. Humphrey debated a long time whether to make the news public himself. He later recalled asking himself "if I should have blown the whistle on Anna Chennault and Nixon." Because he was not sure, and because such a charge would have been seen as an act of last-minute desperation, Humphrey said nothing about it to reporters. He later won praise for his decency; Nixon won the election.

Election Day, November 5, 1968, brought the long and troubled political process to a climax. The counting of returns stretched well into the early morning of November 6 before a definitive result was reached. Richard Nixon received 31,770,237 votes to 31,270,533 for Humphrey and 9,906,141 for George Wallace. That translated into 43.4

percent for Nixon, 42.7 percent for Humphrey, and 13.5 percent for Wallace. The outcome was more decisive in the electoral college. There Nixon won thirty-two states with 301 electoral votes, Humphrey carried thirteen states and the District of Columbia with 191 electoral votes, and Wallace took five states with 46 electoral votes.

Nixon's electoral majority was a national one. He ran well in the West and Midwest, split the South and border states with Wallace, and carried four states in the Northeast. Because of Wallace's candidacy and Lyndon Johnson's efforts, Nixon lost Texas, but he won other big states such as California, Illinois, New Jersey, Ohio, and Florida. Humphrey's strength was concentrated in the Northeast where he carried Pennsylvania, New York, and Massachusetts. His other large states were Texas and Michigan. He did not do well in the Midwest, where he carried two states, or the Far West, where he also won two states. The Democrats did best in the cities, among black voters, and with union members who resisted the Wallace appeal. Wallace's strength lay in his regional Southern base. He experienced the fate of other third-party candidates who falter when the voters concentrate on the major party hopefuls.

The closeness of the popular vote was deceptive. Four years earlier Lyndon Johnson had received more than 43 million votes against Barry Goldwater. Thus the Democratic total had dropped by nearly 12 million popular votes, a dramatic repudiation of the party in power. Nixon had increased Goldwater's total by more than 4 million votes, and Wallace had taken more than 9 million votes on his own. If the American electorate had cast its ballots for a liberal agenda in 1964, the result four years later suggested a conservative surge and a turning away from activist government.

In the wake of the elections, Democrats looked for reasons to explain their defeat. Party divisions received a large share of the blame. The impact of the national convention, the divisive primary campaigns of the spring, the reluctance of Eugene McCarthy to support Humphrey—all these were cited as reasons for Humphrey's loss. Others assigned Lyndon Johnson part of the responsibility because of his tepid backing of Humphrey and his insistence on adhering to his Vietnam policies for so long.

The two main issues in 1968 were race and the war in Vietnam, but they affected the outcome of the contest in very different ways. The prolonged war in Southeast Asia contributed greatly to the disillusionment with Lyndon Johnson and his party that was so marked in 1968. While the American people had no desire to accept defeat in the war, neither did they wish to bear the cost of an elusive victory after the Tet offensive. As a result, all the candidates took a roughly similar position in which they promised to bring about a satisfactory resolution of the war in a way that would minimize further American losses without humiliation.

The peace issue became significant in the last days of the campaign because of Johnson's proposal for a bombing halt and negotiations. The party and the candidate who seemed most likely to extricate the nation from Vietnam on reasonable terms attracted voter support. The swing to Humphrey upon the announcement of the bombing halt on October 31 gave him a chance to win an election he would otherwise have lost decisively. In the final crisis of his 1968 candidacy, Richard Nixon outmaneuvered Johnson and Humphrey in time to stave off the president's peace initiative.

The 1968 election was not a referendum on the war in Southeast Asia. The candidates blurred their differences over the conflict and found a common ground in promises to pursue negotiations and reduce the American presence in South Vietnam. In this aspect of the campaign Richard Nixon clearly held an advantage. He was without Humphrey's ties to the earlier policy of escalating the war, and he was not obliged to spell out a precise plan for ending the conflict. Although he never said he had a "secret plan" for bringing the war to a conclusion, Nixon fostered the impression that his foreign policy experience and contacts with world leaders would enable him to extricate the United States from the war on more honorable and acceptable terms than Humphrey or Wallace could achieve. Only in the last days of the election, with Johnson's bombing halt, did Nixon's strategy on the war falter. The intransigence of South Vietnam restored the situation in his favor.

The major underlying issue in 1968 was race. It established the context in which the presidential election was played out. The defection of white Democratic voters—in the North to Republican and in the South to Wallace and Nixon—shifted the political balance for Hubert Humphrey and his party. Richard Nixon and the Republicans were the direct beneficiaries of the wedge driven into the Democratic coalition after 1965 by race. Republicans emphasized the legitimate concerns of white and black voters on the problem of crime. Nixon and his party also positioned themselves to assert his respect for the general principle of civil rights while retaining a reluctance to use federal power to compel desegregation in the South or attack racial barriers in the North. The Republican position was a very palatable one to white Democrats who gradually abandoned their traditional party allegiance.

George Wallace was an important contributor to this

process. He provided white Democrats in the South with a reason to leave the party that had been so dominant in their region for decades. His argument that the federal government's racial policies were elitist offered a rationale for opposing Democratic liberalism that became a favored device of Republicans during the 1970s and 1980s. As a result, Hubert Humphrey in 1968 won fewer than 10 percent of the vote among white Southerners. The traditionally secure Democratic base in the South vanished under Wallace's assault; the Republicans inherited his support after 1968.

The election of 1968 thus left the Democrats weakened for a generation. With the South now less hospitable to them, they had to run strongly in the rest of the country to win the electoral votes needed to elect a president. Because of Republican strength in the Plains States and Far West, the Democrats had an almost impossible task to accomplish in winning the White House, as the elections of 1972, 1980, 1984, and 1988 demonstrated. Only in 1976, with the Southerner Jimmy Carter at the head of the ticket, did the Democrats capitalize on Republican division to win back the presidency.

The other chief liability for the Democrats after 1968 was their changed system for selecting presidential nominees. The reformed method of selecting delegates to the national convention, which was put in place after the election, gave considerable power to various interest groups within the party. Satisfying the diverse and quarrelsome Democratic constituencies often resulted in weak nominees, including George McGovern in 1972, Walter Mondale in 1984, and Michael Dukakis in 1988. To avoid the excesses that had helped nominate Humphrey in 1968, the Democrats went too far in the other direction. Despite his flaws as a campaigner, Humphrey was clearly the strongest nominee the

Democrats could have picked in 1968. Fairness in the process rather than the strength of the nominee became the Democratic watchword, at some cost to the party's chances in presidential races.

The advantage gained by Republicans in 1968 became a more enduring ascendancy during the twenty-four years that followed. Under Nixon, the GOP followed policies that attracted Southern whites in great numbers. The "Southern strategy" of grudging enforcement of civil rights undermined the Democrats as potential rivals in presidential races. Jimmy Carter slowed the process in 1976, but the failures of his administration confirmed the Republican advantage. In the 1980s Republican campaigns used the "wedge" issues of race, crime, and national defense to great effect to prevent Democrats from returning to their former home.

To avoid a potential alliance of white and black voters on economic issues, Republican strategy was to emphasize social and cultural questions that would split away whites with conservative views on race, crime, and moral values. An issue such as federal guidelines on busing worked in this way for Nixon in 1968 among Southern whites. Twenty years later Republican campaign chairman Lee Atwater used the issues of Massachusetts prison furloughs and the pledge of allegiance to the American flag to disrupt a possible electoral coalition between poor and middle-class Democrats for Michael Dukakis. Finding the right wedge issue became a standard and finely tuned aspect of Republican campaigns and represented an important legacy of Nixon's campaign in 1968.

The superior financial resources of the GOP in 1968 became another lasting Republican asset. It built its fundraising base among both large and small donors, and used these resources to hone campaign skills which the Democrats did not match. The party unity that Nixon achieved during his 1968 race became typical of Republican performances in presidential elections. The result was a seasoned corps of political operatives for Ronald Reagan and George Bush. As in 1968, the Democrats in contrast always seemed to be organizing their party in the midst of a campaign.

Humphrey's defeat did not threaten the Democratic hold on the House and Senate. Despite Republican gains of five Senate seats and four seats in the House, Democrats remained in control. The Nixon presidency opened an era of divided government in which Republicans usually controlled the presidency while Democrats dominated the House and Senate. The stalemate suited the electorate for two decades until the political gridlock contributed to voter disillusion during the early 1990s. In that sense the 1968 election may well have marked a decisive step in the ongoing deterioration of the American party system at the end of the twentieth century.

The final act of the dramatic events of the 1968 campaign came on January 20, 1969, when Richard Nixon was sworn in as the thirty-seventh president of the United States. For Lyndon Johnson the day marked the end of his public career. He returned to Texas and died four years later in January 1973. Eugene McCarthy left the Senate when his term ended in 1970. He made several other runs for the presidency as an independent candidate but never recaptured the hold on liberal Democrats that made him so formidable during the first half of 1968. Hubert Humphrey was elected to the Senate to succeed McCarthy in 1970 and served there until his death in January 1978. George Wallace ran for president again in 1972, but an assassin's bullet paralyzed him during that campaign. Four years later Jimmy Carter defeated Wallace in the South in the race for the Democratic nomination. Senator Edward M. Kennedy ran for president against Carter in the 1980 Democratic primaries unsuccessfully. The only major contender to emerge from the 1968 campaign with brighter prospects than when he began was Ronald Reagan who was reelected governor of California in 1970, lost a race for the Republican nomination to Gerald Ford in 1976, and then won the White House in 1980.

As for Richard Nixon, the new president in his inaugural address struck a note of conciliation. "In these difficult years, America has suffered from a fever of words, from inflated rhetoric that promises more than it can deliver; from angry rhetoric that fans discontents into hatreds; from bombastic rhetoric that postures instead of persuading. We cannot learn from one another until we stop shouting at one another." Unfortunately, the theme of Nixon's inaugural did not become a trait of his presidency. Despite significant domestic achievements, a foreign policy of détente with the Soviet Union and China, and an end to direct American military involvement in Vietnam, Nixon condoned and participated in illegal acts as president that led to his resignation in August 1974 as a result of the Watergate scandals.

The passions that shaped the violent and turbulent year of 1968, and so influenced the race for the White House, affected American politics for the remainder of the century. The Vietnam War ended in the 1970s, but its pain and divisions still plagued the nation. The race issue remained a major determinant of political results and a source of national discord, as the rioting in Los Angeles in the spring of 1992 indicated.

Writing about the election of 1968, the journalist Theodore H. White commented that "the marvel of American politics previously had been its ability to channel passion into peaceful choice of directions." White's verdict was probably too charitable about earlier elections, but it caught some of the consequences of 1968. He suggested that "in 1968, hate burst out of the channel." American politics was changed for the worse in ways that the nation had not fully absorbed or resolved a quarter of a century after Richard Nixon's narrow victory over Hubert Humphrey.

The victory of Governor Bill Clinton in the 1992 presidential election rested on voter unhappiness with a sluggish economy and the leadership of George Bush. Even then, Clinton was a minority president and the Democrats received less than a majority of the popular vote. The 1992 election gave the Democrats the opportunity to overturn the Republican electoral dominance that was established in 1968. How they handled the nation's problems would determine whether the important political changes of 1968 remained in place or had ended with Clinton's triumph over Ross Perot and George Bush.

Recommended Reading

MUCH OF THIS book is based on original documents at the Lyndon B. Johnson Library in Austin, Texas. This brief essay on published sources is designed to indicate where more information about the people and events discussed can be easily found.

Soon after the 1968 election, journalists published insightful accounts of the contest. Lewis Chester, Godfrey Hodgson, and Bruce Page, *An American Melodrama: The Presidential Campaign of 1968* (New York: Viking, 1969), by three British reporters, is thorough and well written. David English and the Staff of the London *Daily Express, Divided They Stand: The American Election 1968* (Englewood Cliffs, N.J.: Prentice Hall, 1969), is a shorter narrative by another British team. Theodore H. White, *The Making of the President 1968* (New York: Atheneum, 1969), is the analysis of an excellent American reporter. Joe McGinnis, *The Selling of the President 1968* (New York: Trident Press, 1969), examines the Nixon media campaign.

Historical accounts of the year 1968 give most coverage to the Eugene McCarthy and Robert Kennedy campaigns. Charles Kaiser, *1968 in America* (New York: Weidenfeld & Nicolson, 1988), offers a cultural interpretation of the year. Other accounts include David Caute, *The Year of the Barricades: A Journey Through 1968* (New York: Harper and Row, 1988), and Irwin Unger and Debi Unger, *Turning Point: 1968* (New York:

Scribner's, 1988). The best overall treatment of the election itself is Dennis D. Wainstock, "The 1968 Presidential Campaign and Election," Ph.D. dissertation, West Virginia University, 1984.

The central participants in the election left memoirs of their campaigns. Eugene J. McCarthy, *The Year of the People* (Garden City, N.Y.: Doubleday, 1969), reveals why McCarthy inspired so many people in 1968 and also why he lost. Hubert H. Humphrey, *The Education of a Public Man* (New York: Doubleday, 1976), has some fascinating chapters on the election. Richard Nixon, *RN: The Memoirs of Richard Nixon* (New York: Grosset and Dunlap, 1978), often says more than its author intended but requires careful use. Other helpful accounts by participants in the election include Anna Chennault, *The Education of Anna* (New York: Times Books, 1980); Clark Clifford with Richard Holbrooke, *Counsel to the President: A Memoir* (New York: Random House, 1991); and Joseph A. Califano, Jr., *The Triumph and Tragedy of Lyndon Johnson* (New York: Simon and Schuster, 1991).

Among biographies, Arthur Schlesinger, Jr., *Robert Kennedy and His Times* (Boston: Houghton Mifflin, 1978), is thorough and favorable to its subject. Stephen E. Ambrose, *Nixon: The Triumph of a Politician, 1962–1972* (New York: Simon and Schuster, 1989), is a clear account of what Nixon did. Herbert Parmet, *Richard Nixon and His America* (Boston: Little, Brown, 1990), is more sympathetic to Nixon and more analytic than Ambrose. Tom Wicker, *One of Us: Richard Nixon and the American Dream* (New York: Random House, 1991), has several interesting chapters about the 1968 race. Carl Solberg, *Hubert Humphrey: A Political Biography* (New York: W. W. Norton, 1984), treats Humphrey's campaign with insight and thoroughness.

On the ferment over Vietnam in 1968, Charles DeBenedetti and Charles Chatfield, *An American Ordeal: The Antiwar Movement of the Vietnam Era* (Syracuse, N.Y.: Syracuse University Press, 1990), is an admirable synthesis of a large body of

writing about the protest against the war. For accounts of the
election from the perspective of the protesters, see James Miller,
*"Democracy Is in the Streets": From Port Huron to the Siege of
Chicago* (New York: Simon and Schuster, 1987), and Todd
Gitlin, *The Sixties: Years of Hope, Days of Rage* (New York:
Bantam Books, 1987). The best book on the events in Chicago
is David Farber, *Chicago '68* (Chicago: University of Chicago
Press, 1988). Two recent books on the Vietnam War provide
good introductions to that complex question. Gary R. Hess,
Vietnam and the United States (Boston: Twayne, 1990), and
David W. Levy, *The Debate Over Vietnam* (Baltimore: Johns
Hopkins Press, 1991).

For the race issue in 1968 and its long-term impact on
American politics, there are a number of helpful studies.
Michael Barone, *Our Country: The Shaping of America from
Roosevelt to Reagan* (New York: Free Press, 1990), blends
political coverage with election analysis. Thomas Byrne Edsall
and Mary Edsall, *Chain Reaction: The Impact of Race, Rights,
and Taxes on American Politics* (New York: W. W. Norton,
1991), considers how race splintered the Democratic coalition
during the 1960s. Earl Black and Merle Black, *The Vital South:
How Presidents Are Elected* (Cambridge, Mass.: Harvard University Press, 1992), discusses how Republicans made gains
among white Southern voters during the 1960s. Finally, for an
account of money spent on the election of 1968, Herbert
Alexander, *Financing the 1968 Election* (Lexington, Mass.:
D. C. Heath, 1971), is highly useful.

Index

A NOTE ON THE AUTHOR

Lewis L. Gould was born in New York City, studied at Brown University, and received M.A. and Ph.D. degrees from Yale University. He taught briefly at Yale before going to the University of Texas at Austin, where he is now the Eugene C. Barker Centennial Professor in American History. In addition to a great many articles and papers on presidential politics and Western history, Mr. Gould's books include *The Presidency of Theodore Roosevelt*; *Reform and Regulation: American Politics from Roosevelt to Wilson*; and *The Spanish-American War and President McKinley*.